LANDSCAPING with
stone

By Jeanne Huber and the Editors of Sunset Books, Menlo Park, California

SUNSET BOOKS

VICE PRESIDENT, GENERAL MANAGER
  Richard A. Smeby
VICE PRESIDENT, EDITORIAL DIRECTOR
  Bob Doyle
PRODUCTION DIRECTOR
  Lory Day
OPERATIONS DIRECTOR
  Rosann Sutherland
MARKETING MANAGER
  Linda Barker
ART DIRECTOR
  Vasken Guiragossian
SPECIAL SALES
  Brad Moses

STAFF FOR THIS BOOK

MANAGING EDITOR
  Bonnie Monte
SUNSET BOOKS SENIOR EDITOR
  Marianne Lipanovich
WRITER
  Jeanne Huber
COPY EDITOR
  Julie Harris
ILLUSTRATOR
  Rik Olson
PHOTO EDITOR
  Laura Del Fava
PRODUCTION SPECIALIST
  Linda M. Bouchard
PREPRESS COORDINATOR
  Danielle Javier
PROOFREADER
  Joan Beth Erickson
INDEXER
  Barbara J. Braasch

COVER PHOTOGRAPH
Photographer: Saxon Holt.
Landscape designer: Michael Thilgen,
Four Dimensions Landscapes.
COVER DESIGN: Vasken Guiragossian

10 9 8 7 6 5 4 3
First Printing January 2006
Copyright © 2006 Sunset Publishing
Corporation, Menlo Park, CA 94025.

For additional copies of *Landscaping
With Stone* or any other Sunset book,
call 1-800-526-5111 or visit us at
www.sunset.com.

There is tremendous interest these days in incorporating stone into home landscapes. No wonder. Stone is gorgeous. It's the perfect foil for plants of many types. Provided it's installed correctly, stone needs little or no maintenance. And in climates where plants shoot up in spring and then die back over the winter, stone features provide a welcome visual anchor all year. This book explores many options for incorporating stone into a home landscape, and it provides the details necessary to ensure a trouble-free, satisfying installation, whether you do the work yourself or hire someone to do it. You'll also find construction hints for a few situations in which you may be considering man-made materials that resemble stone.

Many experts provided guidance for this book. Particular thanks go to Jim Huber of the Huber & Burton masonry company, Redding, California; Scott Hackney and Lorin Hinton of Marenakos Rock Center, Issaquah, Washington; Craig Powell of Northwest Rock, Kingston, Washington; David Corteau of Stoneyard.com, Littleton, Massachusetts; and Tom Durand of Thomas Durand Stone Masonry, Hudson, Massachusetts.

contents

PATHS, PATIOS, AND STEPS

For paving garden surfaces, no material is more beautiful or durable than natural stone. Already eons old, it gives landscapes a sense of permanence and timelessness. Because stone comes directly from the ground, it roots landscapes to the earth in a way manufactured paving materials cannot match. It stands up to both freezing weather and blazing sun better than manmade materials do. And stone adapts to most any situation.

Depending on the type of stone chosen and how it's installed, the effect can range from quite formal to so informal that the paving looks like part of a natural landscape. A formal path or patio might be created with cut stone set in a precise pattern, broken only by uniform mortar joints. At the other end of the scale is a stepping-stone path surrounded by low-growing thyme, or a boulder-style staircase that forces you to scramble almost as if you were on a mountain hike.

Besides aesthetic issues, there are numerous practical considerations involved in designing the best path, patio, or steps for your garden. Steps, for example, must be built to minimize the danger that someone might trip. And patios, especially those next to buildings, need features that will allow rainwater to drain safely away. These are just two of the issues that this chapter explores.

purposeful paths

In a garden, paths serve the practical purpose of directing traffic and keeping feet out of mud and dust. But they also help determine how people experience the garden. A path can encourage visitors to linger at the spot that has the best view, or it can direct people away from the place where you store trash. By drawing the eye off into the distance, a path can also make a garden seem larger than it is. Changing the paving material as a path moves into different areas of the garden further enhances this illusion. Through tricks such as these, a path adds elements of mystery and adventure to a garden. It invites visitors to explore further.

ABOVE: *Tightly fitted bluestone pavers give this entry a formal yet friendly look and are easy to negotiate and clean. Wider spacing is fine for the side path.*

LEFT: *In a Japanese-style garden, rugged, irregular stepping-stones set high above surrounding gravel create a pathway that encourages people to slow down and leave city hubbub behind.*

ABOVE: *To make a path-way more exciting, vary the way you place the stone. Bluestone pavers set on edge create the illusion of a rock outcrop on a mountain.*

LEFT: *Small stones make wonderful paths when they are arranged artfully. Flagstone pavers team up with round gravel (far left) to create a path rich with texture. A pebble mosaic featur-ing flowers and spirals enlivens a mortared stone path (near left).*

9

stepping-stone paths

nstalling stepping-stones is the minimalist approach to garden paving. This type of path is relatively inexpensive and easy to build. It's also easy on the eye. Setting the stepping-stones doesn't usually require much tampering with the general lay of the land, so the path tends to become one with its surroundings. A stepping-stone path is intended for walking on, rather than, say, pushing a wheelbarrow. Because people must think a bit about where to step, it encourages them to slow down and notice the surroundings.

Stepping-stone paths can tiptoe across water or land, as shown in the photos below. In an artificial pond, concrete footings for the stones must be installed before a liner is spread out; see page 134 for specifics.

LEFT: *A path of stepping-stones and gravel links a beach-side garden with the water.*

BELOW: *Set low enough so a mower can run over it, a stepping-stone path across lawn looks casual and demands little care.*

Design Tip

Have the path meander over, between, under, alongside, and around other garden elements to slow the journey through the garden.

Plan your stepping-stone path to meet your particular needs. For example, add extra stones where people will gather, get in and out of cars, or converge as they near a door to your house.

DESIGNING A STEPPING-STONE PATH

A stepping-stone path should look natural and be easy to use. If the stones are big enough, you can set them in a line. But for an even more pleasing look—and one that matches a person's natural gait—place stones in a subtle zigzag. Alternate pieces so that one is slightly to the right and the next is slightly to the left. Whichever approach you choose, the path will usually look better if you position each stone so that its longest dimen-sion runs across the path, not in the direction people walk.

You can set stepping-stones flush with surrounding soil or elevate them an inch or two. Maintenance issues may help you decide: You can run a lawn-mower over stepping-stones that are set flush, but if you plan to use a string trimmer to cut back plants that creep over stones, elevating the stones helps keep you from cutting back too much. If the path traverses an area that's often wet, elevated stones stay cleaner, too.

Stepping-stone paths generally look best with evenly spaced stones placed so their longest dimension runs across the path, but there are no hard and fast rules. You can double up stones (below left) or orient some lengthwise and some crosswise (below right).

Design Tip

For a natural look, place stepping-stones so they relate to one another. For example, set the straight edge of one stone against a straight edge of the next stone. Place a con-cave edge against a convex edge.

SHOPPING FOR STEPPING-STONES

Although you can use rocks with just one flat face, pieces that are relatively flat on both top and bottom are easier to set. Garden centers and some home centers carry suitable pieces. Stone yards, which are listed in the phone book under "Stone—Natural," have an even wider selection.

TYPES Sedimentary rocks, such as sandstone, bluestone, and slate, were formed in layers and therefore naturally break into the relatively flat pieces that are easiest to use. But don't rule out harder, rougher stones such as granite and basalt. Here are some other issues to consider:

- An irregular surface makes a path more interesting, and it improves traction so people are less likely to slip. But avoid dish-shaped stones: if water puddles in the hollows and freezes, the stepping-stones could become slippery.
- Soft, porous stone, such as sandstone, is likely to become covered with slippery moss if your pathway is damp and shaded. Though fine for a trail that carries the eye into woodland, it might not be best for a path that you intend to use frequently.
- Avoid shale, which resembles slate but breaks down over time. Reputable stone yards don't carry it. If you have layered stone on your property and want to determine whether it's worth using, try splitting a few pieces. Shale usually crumbles, while slate separates into thin layers. Some slate is even hard enough to scratch glass.
- For stepping-stones that blend in with their surroundings, choose local stone where possible. You'll probably save money by doing this as well.

IDEAL SIZES Large stones work best, especially along busy routes. Ideal pieces are at least 18 inches wide and 15 to 18 inches long. Avoid using stones less than 2 inches thick, because they're likely to wobble. If you want elevated stepping-stones, buy pieces that are at least 3 or 4 inches thick.

Many companies allow customers to sort through piles to pick out specific pieces. If your path consists of just a few stones, selecting each one makes sense. But if you have a long route, you might want to focus on picking out a few unusually large stones to anchor the beginning and end of the path and buy the rest by the pallet load.

QUANTITIES Many stepping-stone paths consist of one stone per step. Determining how many you need is simple. Just pace the route, counting your steps as you go. Try to walk as you would when using the path—quick, long strides to a compost pile, for example, but shorter steps on a stroll into the garden.

Crazy granite

Old Town sandstone

Rose Blush

Coldwater Canyon

Three Rivers tumbled

Sonoran Gold

Arizona flagstone, a type of sandstone rich with colors of the desert, pairs perfectly with this adobe-style house and wall. A path like this can widen as it nears a doorway, driveway, or other place where people are likely to linger.

Alternatively, you can purchase stepping-stones by weight. This approach works well if you want to build a path several stones wide and will be buying them by the pallet load without counting individual pieces. Multiply the length and width of your path and divide it by the coverage that the stone yard lists for the material you want to buy. This is the number of tons you would buy if you wanted closely spaced stones. Reduce this number to account for the wider spacing on stepping-stone paths.

A stepping-stone 18 inches square by 4 inches thick weighs about 120 pounds, which means you may get 15 to 20 pieces per ton. A ton of these rocks is about half a pallet load, or a pile about 18 inches high on a base 40 by 48 inches.

TRADE SECRET

If you're working with a landscaping plan drawn up by a professional, be aware that individual stepping-stones may not be drawn to scale. Choose stone you like. Then calculate the number of pieces you need based on the dimensions of the path. The staff at the stone yard can help you.

BUILDING A STEPPING-STONE PATH

Building a stepping-stone path is often one of those rare projects that you can begin right away. If you want to surround the stones with pebbles or new plants, you will need to clear the entire path area first, but avoid digging too deep because you'll need to replace disturbed soil under the stones with gravel or sand. If the stepping-stones cross lawn, a flower bed, or woods, there is no prep work at all. Simply outline the general route with garden hoses and begin arranging the stones. You can place stepping-stones directly on soil, but using a sand base makes it easier to set them so they don't wobble.

If your pathway crosses an area that is especially damp, or if you live where spring thaws tend to buckle the soil surface, install 4 to 8 inches of gravel beneath the stepping-stones to help ensure good drainage.

If stepping-stones run up or down a slope, plan your project more as if you were building stairs (see page 82). Rest the front edge of each higher step on the back edge of the stepping-stone below.

LAYING STEPPING-STONES IN SOIL OR SAND

Set stepping-stones so the top surface is 1 or 2 inches above surrounding soil. This will help keep mud off the path.

Rough-textured stepping-stones rise above a pine needle mulch, which extends into the adjoining flower beds. Besides keeping down weeds, the decorative mulch helps unify the path and garden.

1 Place stones along the route so that their longest dimension runs across the path, not in line with it. You may want to set one stone slightly to the right and the next slightly to the left. As you work, walk across stones you have placed to determine the location of the next one.

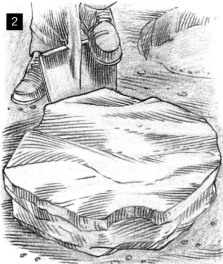

If you want uniform spacing between stones, walk the route first, counting your steps, then divide the total distance by the number of steps to get your stride length. Subtract the space needed for a typical stone and you'll know what gap to leave between stones. Cut a spacer from a scrap of wood so you don't have to measure as you set each stone.

2 Cut around the first stone with a spade, knife, edging tool, or brick set to mark the shape. Then tip the stone on an edge and roll it to the side.

3 Excavate the hole. Cut edges straight down, using a straight-edged spade or a brick set with a hammer, then remove soil within the outline. Make the hole half as deep as the stone is thick plus 1 inch to allow for a sand base. (For example, a stone 4 inches thick needs a hole at least 3 inches deep so that half the stone will be embedded.) Remove all loose soil, even if the hole becomes deeper.

4 Spread 1 inch of sand (more if the hole is extra deep). Dampen with a fine spray of water. Tip the stone back into place. Twist it into the sand until the stone is level and firm.

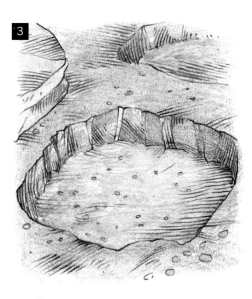

5 Add more sand around the stone and pack the edges. Water with a fine spray to settle the sand. Add more sand as needed to finish setting the stone. Repeat these steps for the remaining stones.

LAYING STEPPING-STONES IN LAWN

Across lawn, you may want to set stepping-stones flush with the soil so they don't interfere with mowing.

Follow the same basic procedure as you would to build a pathway across soil. But once you've cut around each stone, peel back the turf inside the outline, using a flat spade or knife to sever the roots. Excavate a hole that's at least 1 inch deeper than the stone. Then add the sand base and settle the stone into place.

RIGHT: *Exposed aggregate pavers—concrete squares with pebbles on the surface—march on the diagonal.*

LAYING STEPPING-STONES IN GRAVEL

If you have an existing gravel path, you can create a more solid walkway by adding stepping-stones. Follow the procedure for laying stones in soil or sand. Use a small pry bar to loosen packed gravel within the holes.

To build this type of path from scratch, follow the steps for building a gravel path on pages 28–29. Place the stepping-stones on the packed, crushed gravel. Then fill in around them with decorative gravel, stopping 1 or 2 inches below the top of the stones.

Wide spacing and relatively small stepping-stones make this path seem more like a gravel walkway that happens to have solid pieces to keep your feet from sinking in.

Moving Heavy Pieces

Avoid lifting a heavy stone into position whenever possible so you don't hurt your back. Drag, roll, tip, or pry it instead. When you absolutely must lift, squat down and grab hold of the stone; then, keeping your back straight and the stone close to your body, lift with your legs.

- To move a heavy stone with a wheelbarrow, tip the wheelbarrow on its side and roll the stone in. Then walk around so you're facing the underneath side of the wheelbarrow. Wedge your foot against the wheel and tip the wheelbarrow upright.

- Try a hand truck or a two-wheel garden cart, which you can load simply by rolling a stone into position. Or rent a boulder cart, shaped to keep stones from rolling off.

- Tip the stone onto a piece of ¾-inch-thick plywood, and use a series of round poles underneath as rollers.

- To fine-tune a stone's placement, use a pry bar or a rock bar (a thick iron bar with a handle at least 4 feet long). The longer the handle, the easier the job. For a fulcrum, slip a small rock or a sturdy piece of wood underneath the bar close to where it contacts the rock. Don't get your fingers between the bar and the rock.

- Consider using a come-along, a cable-ratcheting device. Wrap a sturdy chain securely around the stone, with padding slipped underneath to avoid chipping the surface or scraping off moss. Hook on one end of the come-along to the chain. Hook the other end to a chain wrapped around a sturdy tree (with padding to protect the bark) or to a vehicle. Slowly ratchet up the tension to move the stone. Be sure to obey the manufacturer's safety precautions. When the cable is taut, check to see that the stone is moving. If it's not, you are merely stretching the cable, which could cause it to slip—a dangerous situation. Use another method to move the stone.

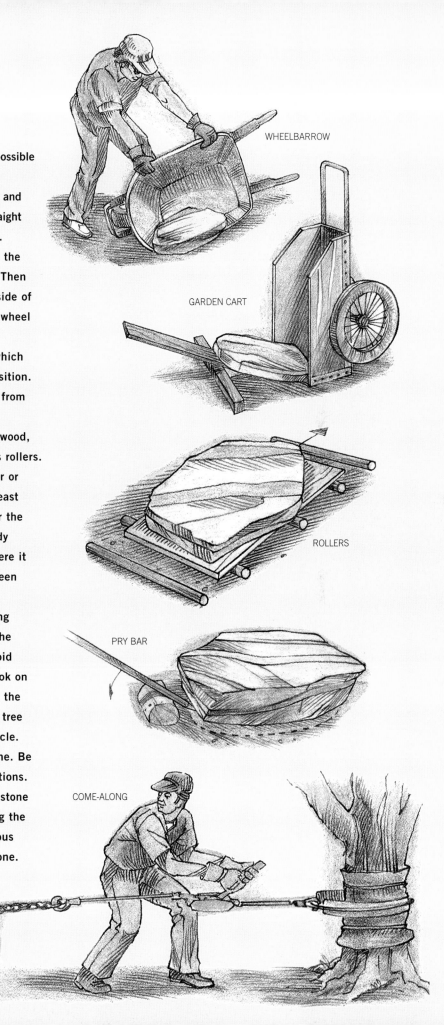

WHEELBARROW

GARDEN CART

ROLLERS

PRY BAR

COME-ALONG

PLANTING BETWEEN STEPPING-STONES

Finding plants that will grow between stepping-stones isn't as tricky as it is with other types of stone pathways. Spaces around the stones are usually generous enough to give most plant roots what they need, assuming you loosen and amend the soil as you would when planting elsewhere.

But you do need to pick plants that are sturdy enough to withstand at least occasional foot traffic and compact enough so no one will trip. Because stepping-stones invite people to place their feet deliberately, you can include plants that send up flower stalks that people will have to step over; just be aware that this will slow travel and might not be the best situation for a busy path. For a fragrant path, choose plants that release sweet-smelling oils when the leaves are crushed.

Plants rated for at least light foot traffic, such as silver carpet, often thrive between stepping-stones because the stones absorb most of the impact. Select plants whose water needs match those of plants in nearby beds.

Garden Thugs

Plants that thrive in stone walkways must be tough. Unfortunately, that means they're also likely to grow vigorously where you don't want them. Check with your local Cooperative Extension Office or a good nursery to learn whether the plants you're considering are pests in your area. Be especially cautious if your path is close to a natural area. It's far easier to eradicate a pest plant in a small garden than it is in a field or forest.

Besides considering the plants listed here, see pages 50–51 for varieties recommended for flagstone paths. Plants that thrive in those tight spaces should do even better when planted between stepping-stones. Buy small plants and water them regularly until they settle in.

Blue star creeper

Pratia pedunculata / Hardy to –7°F/ –22°C. Sun, but part shade in hot areas. Regular water. Occasional foot traffic. This creeper grows just 2–3 inches tall. Its tiny leaves resemble those of baby's tears *(Soleirolia soleirolii)*. Pale blue, starlike flowers appear in late spring and summer.

Carpet bugle

Ajuga reptans / Hardy to –40°F/–40°C. Sun or partial shade. Regular water. Light foot traffic. Shiny oval leaves sprout flower spikes in spring; most types have blue flowers. *A. reptans* spreads by runners, so it's likely to show up in nearby lawn. *A. genevensis* does not form runners, but it's taller and works only along path edges.

Blue star creeper

Chamomile

Chamaemelum nobile (Anthemis nobilis) / Hardy to −30°F/−34°C. Sun or partial shade. Moderate water, but can withstand some drought. Moderate foot traffic. Bright green leaves form a soft mat 3–12 inches tall. Mow after bloom. 'Treneague', a nonflowering type, doesn't need deadheading and won't draw bees.

English daisy

Bellis perennis / Hardy to −30°F/−34°C. Sun, but light shade in hot areas. Moderate to lots of water. Some foot traffic. Flowers, on stems up to 6 inches tall, may be pink, rose, red, or white. This is the tiny, daisylike plant that often appears in lawn. Self-seeds freely.

Korean grass

Zoysia tenuifolia / Hardy to −7°F/−22°C. Sun, but tolerates some shade. Regular water. Heavy foot traffic. Mow 1–2 inches high for a mossy look, or leave it to grow to its mature height of 9–10 inches to create a bumpy look.

Miniature daisy

Bellium minutum / Hardy to 10°F/−12°C. Full sun, but part shade in hotter climates. Regular water. Moderate foot traffic. Tiny white daisies with yellow centers cover lime green leaves that form mats 3–6 inches tall. Blooms nearly year-round where winters are mild. Self-seeds.

New Zealand brass buttons

Leptinella squalida (formerly *Cotula squalida*) / Hardy to 0°F/−18°C. Sun or partial shade. Normal water. Moderate foot traffic. Feathery leaves form a mat

Carpet bugle

Chamomile

English daisy

3–6 inches tall that spreads quickly by runners. Tiny, yellowish green flowers resemble buttons.

Pussy toes

Antennaria dioica / Hardy to −40°F/−40°C. Full sun. Moderate to regular water. Light foot traffic. Woolly gray leaves form inch-high mats; pinkish white

puffs of flower blooms, on stems several inches tall. A good choice for paths that are in bright sun and rather dry.

Silver carpet

Dymondia margaretae / Hardy to 0°F/−18°C. Full sun to light shade. Moderate to regular water. Light foot traffic. Grayish green mat 2–3 inches tall bears yellow daisylike flowers in summer. Established plants are fairly drought tolerant.

Speedwell

Veronica liwanensis / Hardy to −7°F/−22°C. Full sun. Little water. Light foot traffic. Use ground-hugging types of veronicas between stepping-stones. *V. liwanensis* is covered with bright blue flowers in spring. A similar kind of speedwell, *V. repens,* has tiny lavender to white flowers in spring; it tolerates some shade, slightly colder temperatures, and a bit more water than *V. liwanensis.*

Woolly yarrow

Achillea tomentosa / Hardy to −40°F/−40°C. Full sun. Little to moderate water. Occasional foot traffic. Tough carpet of fernlike leaves has tall, flat clusters of bright yellow to cream-colored flowers in summer. Shear to remove spent flowers. Drought tolerant once established.

gravel paths

Listen as you stroll a gravel path, and the stones will reveal their identity. If they crunch, they're probably round stones all about the same size. But if they're mum, the pieces are almost certainly crushed stone of varying sizes. The talkative path will stay loose underfoot for years. The silent one has probably already been packed hard—a useful trait if you plan to run a wheelbarrow over it. Gravel paths are inexpensive and easy to build. They never become slippery, nor are they likely to create rainwater runoff problems. Gravel can also lend a certain country charm to a landscape.

Even in damp shade (facing page) gravel is never slippery. As both mulch and paving material (below), it blends a path and a flower bed.

ABOVE: *A gravel path contrasts beautifully with water-thrifty plants, whether they are prairie natives (top) or a more eclectic mix, such as spiky New Zealand flax and plume-topped pampas grass (bottom). Check with a local nursery before planting pampas grass, which is invasive in some areas.*

23

DESIGNING A GRAVEL PATH

A gravel path can be curved or straight, narrow or wide. Because there's no need to shape individual stones or to accommodate their existing sizes, your design isn't as limited as it is with other types of stone paving. However, there are certain issues you should take into consideration as you lay out the path:

- Although 2 feet is considered the minimum width, two people need a path 5 feet wide if they are to walk side by side. Provide an even wider area if you wish to showcase garden plants that thrive in the microclimate gravel creates (see pages 30–31).

- Gravel stays put only on relatively flat stretches. If your site slopes, choose another paving material, or break the path into a series of terraces.

- Consider maintenance issues as you fine-tune the route. A path in the open usually needs monthly raking or blowing to keep it free of needles and leaves; if the path crosses under messy plants, the gravel will need more frequent cleaning.

- Gravel may catch on shoes and be carried indoors, where it can scratch the floor. To guard against damage, you may need to design your path with a wide landing of stone or concrete—or plan to institute a "shoes off" policy indoors. You also may want to confine gravel to secondary paths, rather than use it for the main route to your house. Or you can settle stepping-stones into the gravel (see page 18).

You can buy pebbles that are basically all one color or opt for a multicolored mix, as the builder of this path did.

Gravel in a mixture of sizes and colors provides a textured look. If you plan to clean your path with a rake, make sure all pieces are small enough to slip between the tines. If you will be using a blower, you can use larger pieces.

A path of decomposed granite packs down so firmly that you can sweep away any leaves or debris.

ADDING A STABILIZER

If you're worried that gravel might migrate into your garden or house, you may want to spray it with an acrylic or vinyl acetate soil stabilizer.

Stabilizer binds the gravel to the path. It stiffens the surface, making it more suitable for someone in a wheelchair, and it causes the path to shed rainwater, which reduces the chance that weed seeds might grow in the path. Stabilizer remains flexible enough, however, that it can be used in areas with very cold winters.

But there are a few caveats. Stabilizer won't work on round gravel. You must use crushed gravel that includes fine particles. Gravel ¼ inch or smaller works best, but you can use pieces up to ¾ inch. Stabilizer may also leave the path looking a bit plastic-coated, so be sure to test a sample patch first. And, because the stabilizer causes water to run off, you must design the path's drainage just as you would if the surface were solid pavement. Slope the gravel at least ½ inch per 4 feet (or tip it toward the side by this amount), and plan where the runoff will go.

PROVIDING FOR LAYERS

If you are using crushed gravel, you can fill the entire area you excavate with it. But sometimes it makes more sense to have two or three layers of different types:

- If you select a type of gravel that's unusually expensive, save money by using it only for the top couple of inches and use less expensive gravel underneath.
- If you're worried about drainage, fill the bottom of the excavation with ¾-inch gravel, and order it without fine particles so water can fill the spaces between pieces. Put smaller gravel with "fines" on top. Place landscape fabric between the layers so the fine particles don't wash into the bottom gravel and clog it.
- If you want round pebbles on the surface, use crushed gravel on the bottom and add only a couple of inches of the round pebbles. Otherwise, the path will be hard to walk on.

Design Tip

Place a solid stone apron at the doorstep so that gravel doesn't travel on people's shoes into the house, where it might scratch floors.

A single type of edging unifies a paved area with a gravel path that leads off into the garden. Gravel is ideal for branch paths like this one.

SHOPPING FOR GRAVEL

Gravel for paths comes in white, black, green, red, and brown, round and crushed, as well as in different sizes. The type or types you choose make a big difference in the overall effect.

Although you can buy gravel by the bag at most stores that sell building materials, you'll save money and find a better selection by purchasing material by the cubic yard or ton from stone yards or other companies that stock decorative gravel in bulk.

SPECIFICATIONS It's possible to install a gravel path on an excavation just 3 inches deep. But the path will drain better and be much easier to maintain if you go down at least 6 to 8 inches. If the soil is soggy, use a 3-inch-deep layer of ¾-inch crushed gravel as a base, and then top that with the gravel of your choice.

If you want a path that crunches and is loose underfoot, the top surface should consist of natural or beach gravel, also known as pea gravel. Gravel of this type consists of rounded stones that are all one size, or "neat." Diameters of ⅜, ½, or ⅝ inch work well.

For a silent path, get crushed gravel that includes fine particles. The sharp edges of the gravel interlock, and the small particles fill spaces, creating a firm mass. Specify the maximum size and add the word "minus" to your request to indicate that you want smaller particles included. A ⅝-minus mix, for example, consists of pieces that range down from ⅝ inch in diameter. For a smoother surface, choose smaller gravels. Both ¼-minus gravel and decomposed granite, a very fine by-product of granite min-

ing, pack down to look and feel almost like pavement; either is an excellent choice if you will be running wheelbarrows, bicycles, or carts down the path.

With both round and crushed gravel, avoid getting pieces with a diameter larger than ¾ inch. These are difficult to walk on.

ESTIMATING QUANTITIES Calculating quantities is easy in theory—just multiply the width, length, and depth of the path. But dealing with inches, feet, and yards complicates the math. The easiest method is to convert everything to either feet or inches and then do the multiplying.

- If you use feet, divide the resulting number by 27 and you will have the cubic yards needed for your project.
- If you use inches, convert to cubic yards by dividing by 46,656 (the equivalent of dividing by 12 three times in a row, then by 27).

In truth, you can skip the calculations entirely. The gravel company's staff will do the math for you if you tell them the dimensions of your project. Consider ordering 5 to 10 percent extra to be sure you don't run short.

Gravel comes in many textures and colors. Clockwise from top: Quartz, La Paz (a kind of river-rounded granite), ¼-inch dolomite, ¾-inch red lava, tumbled Japanese riverstone, ¼-inch pea gravel, aqua cove mix, ⁵⁄₁₆-inch red lava.

Adding Edging

Gravel paths require edging material, and most other stone pathways benefit from it as well. Besides helping to lock the paving into place, edging material often contributes significantly to the overall appeal of a path. Some edging is barely noticeable—a good choice if you want to create an illusion that your path is winding naturally across a site. The following types of edging work with a variety of paving materials:

CUT STONE set on edge creates an especially elegant look. Set the top edge so it will extend 1 or 1½ inches above the gravel or other paving material. Butt the edging pieces tightly. If you are using mortar between joints on the path, use it between edging pieces as well.

BRICKS provide a traditional touch that's equally at home in a formal garden or one with a cottage feel. Stand bricks on end, "soldier" style, or place pieces at a 45-degree angle.

METAL is tidy and unobtrusive. Use metal strips fabricated as edging. Or buy ⅛-inch by 4-inch flat stock (used by blacksmiths) from an iron supply company and pin it in place with rebar about 12 inches long.

PLASTIC EDGING is available at masonry supply stores in several styles. For gravel paths, get rolls with a wide, rounded top edge. For stone paving at least 1½ inches thick, look for the type designed for brick paving (shown in the illustration).

WOOD OR COMPOSITES of plastic and wood fiber also make attractive edging. Wood should be either naturally rot-resistant (such as the dark-colored heartwood of cedar or redwood) or pressure-treated with preservatives. For curves, use benderboard, which is about ⅜ inch thick, or a flexible type of composite lumber.

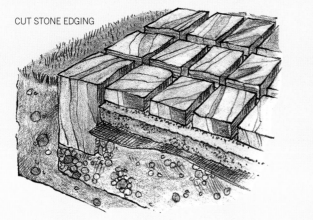

CUT STONE EDGING

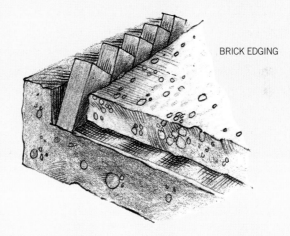

BRICK EDGING

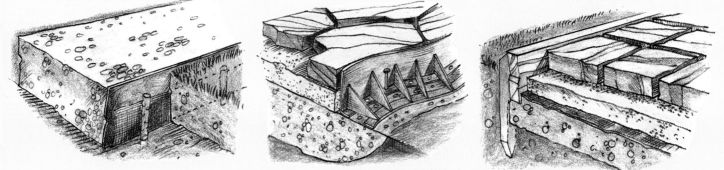

METAL EDGING

PLASTIC EDGING

WOOD EDGING

BUILDING A GRAVEL PATH

With garden hoses, string, or sticks, mark the outline of your path.

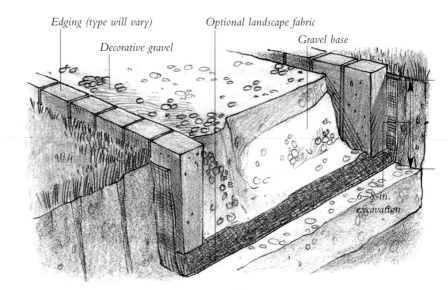

Edging (type will vary)

Decorative gravel

Optional landscape fabric

Gravel base

6–8-in. excavation

1 Excavate the path area to a depth of 6 to 8 inches. If you are using brick or cut stone edging, slice straight down along the perimeter with a spade, and excavate a bit deeper along the edges, if necessary, so that the top of the edging will be 1 to 1½ inches higher than the surrounding soil. Go out a few inches farther if you are using other edging so that you will have room to attach stakes or spikes. If your path crosses lawn, remove the sod with roots intact by slicing horizontally a few inches down and then rolling up sections of turf as if they were carpet. Use a pointed shovel or a spade with its bottom nearly flat to the ground, a hand sod cutter flat on the ground, or a motorized sod cutter. This machine, which can be rented, slices back and forth under the sod at a depth you set. Because it's heavy and prone to bucking around, it needs a strong operator.

2 Install landscape fabric, if you are using it. Cut it wide enough to extend under the edging and perhaps even wrap up the outside almost to the soil line. Overlap pieces by 12 to 18 inches.

3 Install whatever edging you have chosen.

4 Add a 3-inch base of crushed gravel. If the path area has poor drainage, use pieces with a diameter of ¾ inch; if drainage is good, the gravel size isn't critical.

5 Rake the gravel into a uniform layer, then dampen it. Use a fine spray of water to nudge tiny pieces of gravel into crevices between larger particles.

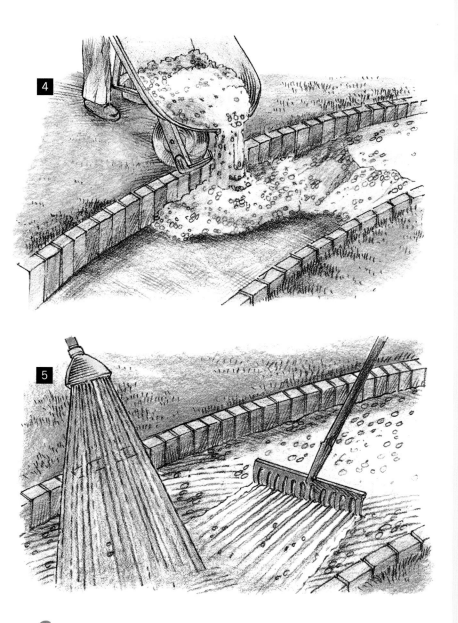

Landscape Fabric: Yes or No?

Many people spread landscape fabric, also known as weed cloth, over the excavated area before they add gravel. While the fabric can keep gravel from sinking into soggy clay, it is no panacea for stopping weeds.

Landscape fabric blocks only sprouts and runners that might come up from below; it doesn't prevent seeds that land on the surface from sprouting (and sometimes growing down into the cloth, where they're harder to remove).

You can prevent weed growth just as effectively by building your path thick enough to block sunlight from the soil, and keeping the path clean of leaves and needles. Without decaying organic matter to nourish them, any seeds that land on the gravel and sprout will probably die on their own. If they don't, pull them by hand while they're still small. Otherwise, loosen the gravel with a pick and remove the weeds, roots and all.

6 After any standing water has disappeared, pass over the area with a hand tamper several times to pack the gravel firmly. If you have a long, straight path, you can use a motorized plate compactor instead, but switch to the hand tamper along edges.

Add enough gravel to make another 3-inch-deep layer, and repeat Steps 5 and 6. Add any remaining gravel and repeat, but skip the final tamping if you are using round gravel for the top layer and want to hear it crunch as you use your path.

PLANTING IN GRAVEL

An expanse of gravel may look forlorn, but it can actually yield one of the most interesting planting situations in your garden. Gravel creates a microclimate far different from that in standard garden beds. By expanding your gravel path to create planting areas, or by building an independent gravel garden, you may be able to grow plants that would otherwise fail in your climate. Gravel can, for example, trick a plant adapted to the arid West into thriving even in the rainy East or Northwest by draining water away from the crown. Gravel also helps plants adapted to moist climates survive in arid regions even with relatively little irrigation. It acts as mulch, keeping soil moisture from evaporating.

Fragrant herbs and other drought-tolerant plants from the Mediterranean and similar regions grow well in gravel that isn't packed too hard or deep.

A gravel garden can also be planted to create a fair facsimile of a beach. If you live along an actual beach, investigate the plants that grow naturally in your area; they generally will perform best and are likely to provide the best food and cover for birds and other wildlife.

Besides the following plants, consider the ones with low water needs listed on pages 20–21 and 50–51.

Fragrant lavender, native to the Mediterranean, thrives in gravel that isn't packed too hard or deep.

Adam's needle

Yucca filamentosa / Hardy to –60°F/ –51°C. Full sun. Little to moderate water. Adam's needle has the same large, sword-shaped leaves and beautiful flowers as other yuccas, but it tolerates a wider range of conditions. Fragrant flowers appear on stalks up to 7 feet tall in late spring or early summer.

Adam's needle

Coreopsis

Beard tongue

Penstemon / Hardiness varies. Sun, but part shade in hot areas. Little to moderate water. Penstemons have narrow, bell-shaped flowers, typically in reds and blues. *P. barbatus,* from the Southwest, and *P. digitalis,* from the eastern and central states, tolerate heat and humidity.

Coreopsis

Hardy to –20°F/–29°C. Full sun. Little to moderate water. Choose tough perennial forms, such as *C. grandiflora,* which grows 1–2 feet tall and is covered with bright yellow flowers, or *C. auriculata* 'Nana', with orange-yellow flowers above foliage just 5–6 inches tall.

Evening primrose (sundrops)

Oenothera / Hardy to –22°F/–30°C. Full sun, but part shade in hot areas. Little to moderate water. Related to the dune primroses found near many beaches. Evening primroses feature flowers in bright yellow, pink, or white. Many open in late afternoon. Ozark sundrops *(O. macrocarpa)* is native to the south-central United States; *O. fruticosa* is native to the eastern United States.

Rockrose

Fountain grass

Pennisetum / Hardy to −24°F/ −31°C. Sun or light shade. Moderate to regular water. Long, narrow blades arch gracefully in a fountain shape and move with the wind, just as grasses do on a beach.
P. orientale, which grows 2 feet tall and 2½ feet wide, is a good choice because it rarely self-seeds.

Lavender

Lavandula / Hardiness varies. Full sun. Moderate water. Wands of purple flowers poke out from fragrant gray-green foliage. English lavender *(L. angustifolia)* prefers having its feet in gravel rather than moist garden soil; it's hardy to −10°F/ −23°C. Spanish lavender *(L. stoechas)* is a bit less cold tolerant, and French lavender *(L. dentata)* is even pickier. Plant lavender out of main pathways so you won't have to dodge bees.

Mount Atlas daisy

Anacyclus depressus / Hardy to −34°F/ −37°C. Full sun. Little to moderate water. This member of the aster family forms a mat of grayish, lacy leaves. Daisylike flowers 2 inches across appear during the summer.

Sage

Rockrose

Cistus / Hardy to 10°F/−12°C. Full sun. Little or no water. From spring into early summer, these carefree shrubs are covered with flowers that resemble single roses. White rockrose *(C. × hybridus)* reaches 3–4 feet tall and 4–8 feet wide. Orchid rockrose *(C. × purpureus)* stays under 4 feet in both dimensions.

Sage

Salvia / Hardy to −37°F/−38°C. Full sun. Regular water. This enormous family of plants includes common sage *(S. officinalis),* the culinary staple. Depending on the type, common sages grow 1–3 feet tall and 1–1½ feet wide.

Switch grass

Panicum virgatum / Hardy to −20°F/ −29°C. Full sun to light shade. Little to ample water. This perennial, native to

Switch grass

Midwest prairies, forms tall clumps of leaves that rustle in the wind. Loose flower clusters reach as high as 7 feet.

Verbena

Verbena canadensis / Hardy to −10°F/ −23°C. Full sun. Moderate water. This low-growing, spreading perennial has rose-purple blooms for most of the summer from Virginia to Florida west to Colorado and Mexico. The species form grows 1½ feet tall; some varieties are only 6 inches. Usually grown as an annual.

Yarrow

Achillea / Hardy to −30°F/−34°C. Full sun. Little to moderate water. These easy-care plants have feathery leaves, topped in summer by clusters of long-lasting flowers. Choices range from ground-hugging woolly yarrow *(A. tomentosa)* to 3-foot-tall common yarrow *(A. millefolium)* and 4–5-foot-tall fernleaf yarrow *(A. filipendulina).*

Yarrow

mixing stone and concrete

If you love the look of a path covered with small stones but want something more solid to walk on, consider building a path of concrete that has pebbles or flat stones exposed on the surface.

EXPOSED AGGREGATE

For the look of a gravel path, create a finish known as exposed aggregate. Simply brush away the surface skim on ordinary concrete before it sets, which reveals the gravel within the mixture. Or you can add extra pebbles to the surface before the concrete sets. The second method is more common because it allows you to use decorative pebbles to dress up standard concrete.

With either method, the first steps are the same as they would be if you were pouring an ordinary concrete path. Assuming you want a straight path, build wooden forms from 2 by 4s over a gravel base. The setup is similar to the bottom layer of a gravel path (see page 29). Make path sections no more than 10 feet long. This helps prevent shrinkage cracks.

Use bagged concrete mix, plus about ½ gallon of extra Portland cement per bag. Or make your own mix from 1 part Portland cement to 2 parts pea gravel (⅜-inch diameter or less) and 2 parts sand, plus about

As an alternative to pouring a path or patio of concrete and then giving the slab an exposed aggregate finish, you can make or buy paver-size pieces with this surface. Install them as you would cut stone (see pages 64 to 67).

½ part water. Pour this mixture into the form and level the surface. Wait for any surface water to disappear.

If you are using decorative pebbles, broadcast them over the surface liberally. Press them in with a magnesium float and then gently trowel the surface to bring up the surface "cream" of cement and fine sand. Trowel just until the pebbles are covered with the cream.

Finishing the process is the same whether you have added decorative pebbles or are just trying to expose gravel within the concrete: When the concrete is stiff, perhaps 6 hours later, brush off the surface with a broom, a nylon scrub brush, or a wire brush, depending on how stiff the concrete has become. Clean away debris using a fine mist from a hose or with a damp masonry sponge, rinsed frequently.

COMBINING LARGER STONES AND CONCRETE

To achieve an exposed-aggregate look using larger stones, you'll need to set the stones in mortar over concrete. Select and arrange the stones for a manageable section (maybe 4 feet square). Mark the stones and move them to the side. If you are covering old concrete, clean it thoroughly and allow it to dry.

When you're ready to mortar in the stones, brush the concrete with bonding adhesive, which resembles white glue, or with a slurry of cement and water. (If you are working with new concrete, you can skip this step. Merely dampen the concrete instead.)

Thoroughly dampen the stones and allow excess water to drain. Working quickly, prepare a mortar mix or a homemade batch of 1 part masonry cement to 3 parts sand, plus just enough water for a stiff mix. Spread it over the concrete and trowel it into a layer at least 1 to 2 inches deep.

Place the stones back in position, as shown above left. To seat them evenly, press them in with a 2 by 4 or a piece of plywood large enough to straddle several stones, shown above right. Wait several hours, then spread a thinner layer of mortar over the surface to fill voids. Wipe away smears with a damp cloth.

Flat, smooth stones make the best candidates for embedding in mortar.

pebble mosaics

Pebble mosaics are the ultimate in exposed aggregate surfaces. Arranged in precise geometric patterns or other designs, the pebbles seem almost like delicate jewels. But the paving is actually very durable because the stones are packed tightly together and set into a base of cement and sand. They're usually set vertically, not flat, making the stonework quite dense. Even with no cement, pebble mosaics in many areas of Europe, Africa, and Asia have survived for centuries.

Mosaics can create an orderly feeling or one of wild abandon. The paving in the courtyard below is faithful to the Muslim tradition that favors geometric designs rather than representations of people or animals. The swirling path (right) by pebble mosaic expert Maggy Howarth was designed to symbolize freedom and energy.

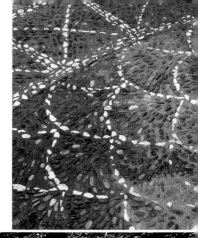

Like stitches in a quilt, single-file white rocks create a repeating pattern (right). Although stone seems an unlikely medium for creating daisies and delicate curlicues (below), this garden is proof that it can be done with flair.

TRADE SECRET

If you've ever collected rocks on a beach, you know that the colors are most vibrant when the pieces are damp. In a path, you can make stones look perpetually moist by coating them with a stone sealer with "wet look" on the label. Or leave the stones unsealed and celebrate the fleeting pleasure of how rainfall transforms your stonework.

MAKING PEBBLE MOSAICS

Mosaic artists generally use pebbles with rounded edges, but you can also incorporate slices of slate, pieces of tile, or other materials. Some landscaping and gravel companies sell pebbles sorted by size and color.

Pebble mosaics are fun to make, but they're more time consuming than you might expect. Limit your first project to no more than 2 or 3 feet square.

Draw a full-size pattern and gather enough stones to carry it out. Stones must be placed with their longest dimension upright, so you will use many more pieces than you may expect.

1 Mark the perimeter, then excavate. Go down 7 inches where winters are mild or 12 inches where soil freezes. Depending on the type of edging (see page 27), install it now or after you have added some or all of the gravel base. Use ⅝-inch crushed gravel with finer

Mixture of sand, cement, and finely crushed rock   *Pebbles*   *Edging (type will vary)*

7–12 in. excavation   *Gravel base (thickness will vary)*

particles included. Spread a 3-inch layer, then spray with water. Tamp the gravel down thoroughly with a hand tamper. Repeat until there is enough space between the gravel and the top of the edging for the longest stones to stand upright with at least ½ inch to spare.

2 If you are attempting a large mosaic, install dividers so that you don't work in areas larger than you can complete that day. From ¼-inch plywood, cut out patterns that match key elements of your design. You can set stones freehand, but patterns will speed the work and pro-

duce better results. Wearing a dust mask and goggles, mix 1 part Portland cement, 2 parts ¼-inch crushed gravel (with or without smaller particles), and 3 parts sand. Fill all but the top ¾ inch within the form with this mixture.

3 Set the patterns onto the sand–cement mixture. Starting next to the patterns, embed pebbles partway into the sand-cement mixture. Pieces must touch each other and have their longest dimension vertical. When you wedge the final piece into place, the stones will become more stable.

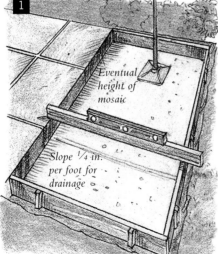

Eventual height of mosaic

Slope ¼ in. per foot for drainage

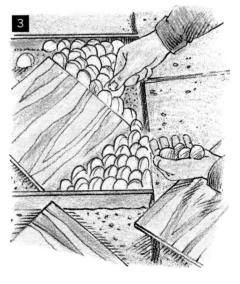

4 Remove the patterns and fill in the remaining areas. Then place a straight board across the form and tap it down to seat the stones evenly. Repeat this across the entire mosaic (or the area you are completing that day).

5 Wearing a dust mask, thoroughly mix 1 part Portland cement and 3 parts fine sand (or used a bagged sand-cement mixture). Sprinkle it over the mosaic and brush it into all crevices.

6 Mist with water. Use a garden sprayer rather than a hose so you don't create puddles or wash away the sand. If holes appear, add more of the sand-cement mixture and mist again. Cover with plastic and anchor all edges with wood or stones. Lift the plastic periodically and spray with water for at least four days. Waiting four weeks is even better; the cement will continue to harden, provided it never dries out during that time.

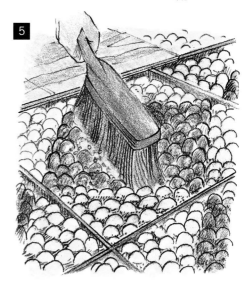

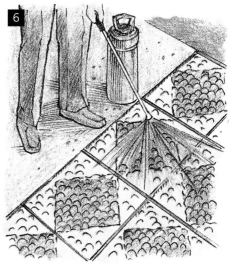

LEFT: *Pebble mosaics about 2 feet square can be used like pavers to create pathways or even patios.*

flagstone paths

The term "flagstone" refers to any stone that naturally occurs in big, flat pieces. Because these are exactly the qualities needed for building stable, easily traveled paths, it's no wonder that this type of stone is one of the most popular paving options. Flagstone serves equally well in a formal entry path that leads directly to a front door or in a meandering route that leads out into a backyard garden. In a formal situation, you might opt to give the path a concrete base so you can fill the joints with mortar. But in a more relaxed setting, you might decide on a sand base and wider spaces so that you can tuck in low-growing fragrant herbs or splashy flowers.

The type of stone plays a major role in the appearance of a flagstone path, but joint details also matter. Meandering, mortar-filled joints (facing page) look casual. Clustered flagstones used like stepping-stones (below) convey an arty, designer touch. At right, the path with more textured stones and plant-filled joints (top) fits an unfussy, country garden, while the one with smoother stones and crisp joints (bottom) suits a garden where everything is kept very tidy.

DESIGNING FLAGSTONE PATHS

In some ways, a flagstone path is simply a grown-up version of a stepping-stone path. But instead of marching as individuals, the stones work together as a team. Because flagstones cover virtually the entire surface, without the wide gaps present in a stepping-stone path, they are suitable for a heavily traveled route or one that needs to support a wheelbarrow or cart. You have several key design choices to make.

The path at left is wide enough that it can be traveled easily even when plants cascade over its edges.

If flowers and greenery will spill over the edges of your path, consider using large stones down the center and filling in along the edges with smaller pieces, known as steppers. This puts the large pieces, which look more substantial, where you will see them year-round. The contrasting sizes create an interesting design to enjoy when edge plants die back during the winter.

If your path is particularly wide, consider placing the largest stones along the edges instead. A path built this way, with smaller stones filling in down the center, creates a strong design statement.

You can set the stones over a base of gravel and sand and fill the joints with either sand or a mixture of sand and cement. Or you can lay the stones on wet mortar over a concrete base and fill the joints with mortar. The following pages explore the factors to consider when choosing between the two methods.

Dense ground cover helps knit relatively small pieces of Arizona sandstone into a stable path. In order to add plants, you must set the stones on a base of finely crushed gravel or sand; you cannot use mortar.

The edge treatment can also vary. If you are setting large flagstones on a base of gravel and sand and plan to plant between them, you might want to forgo edging and let the surrounding soil and plant roots hold the stones in place. But you should probably include edging if the stones are small. In this case, edging will help to hold everything together. You can also opt for edging simply because you like the look. See page 27 for edging ideas.

ABOVE: *Although it generally looks best to set flagstones so their longest dimension runs across a path, in this path the lengthwise orientation conveys a sense of motion and directs people around the curve.*

LEFT: *To make a flagstone path seem like a garden bed, allow extra space between stones and tuck flowering plants into the gaps. This path-garden almost glows with blooms of sweet alyssum and strawflower.*

If you plan to add greenery between flagstones, factor in the growth habits of the plants when you decide which size flagstones to buy. Creeping thyme, shown here, spreads enough to nearly obscure small stones.

SHOPPING FOR FLAGSTONES

You'll find a wide selection of flagstones at most stone yards, from suede-textured sandstone in earthy colors to steel blue slate and glassy quartzite. As long as you buy stone that's thick enough for the construction method you are using, there are no right or wrong choices. But these are some factors to consider:

- If you want a natural-looking path, choose a stone commonly found in your part of the country. Local stone also may be the least expensive.
- If you want a garden filled with desert plants, consider paving with colors of the desert, such as red or buff-colored sandstone. Besides helping to carry out your theme, warm colors contrast beautifully with the gray-green leaves common to water-thrifty plants, as well as with grasses and succulents.
- If your path is in shade or if you live where it is frequently damp, avoid relatively porous stone, such as some types of sandstone. These are likely to quickly become covered with slippery moss. Quartzite, which is basically compressed sandstone, is a better choice.
- If you're planning other garden features made of stone, such as planters or accent boulders, consider what's available for all your projects before deciding on any one component.

Because stone found naturally on a site generally consists of just one type, your garden may look best if you opt for flagstone that's the same basic color as stone you use elsewhere.

SPECIFICATIONS For a flagstone path on a bed of gravel and sand, buy pieces at least 1½ inches thick. Thicker pieces are preferable because the edges wedge together better. For flagstones that will be set in wet mortar, you can use pieces as thin as 1 inch. As for width, you may find flagstones 3 feet across or even larger. Such big slabs look wonderful, but make sure you don't buy pieces too heavy to handle.

Flagstone is generally sold by the ton. Bring the dimensions of your path with you when you shop, and ask the stone yard's staff to calculate how much you need. Buy at least 10 percent extra. To estimate whether a certain type of stone is within your price range, consider that a ton of stone 2 inches thick generally covers about 70 square feet, or about 20 feet of a path that's 3½ feet wide.

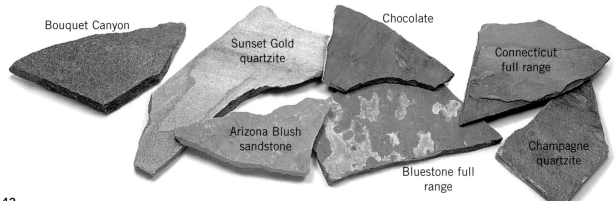

Bouquet Canyon

Sunset Gold quartzite

Chocolate

Connecticut full range

Arizona Blush sandstone

Bluestone full range

Champagne quartzite

ABOVE: *On a color wheel, red and green are opposite each other, which makes them complementary colors. When used together in a design, both colors seem brighter and more intense, as this combination of red Arizona flagstone and Irish moss shows.*

RIGHT: *Built without edging, a dry-laid flagstone path looks almost as informal as if it were made of stepping-stones. Encouraging grass to grow around the stones makes the path easy to maintain and adds to its casual look.*

DECIDING BETWEEN SAND AND MORTAR JOINTS

A dry-laid flagstone path on a bed of gravel and sand with just sand packed into the joints is the simplest type to build. Rainwater filters through reasonably well, so you don't usually need a formal drainage system. The path remains slightly flexible, so the surface is more forgiving if a tree root or ice pushes up from underneath. If the stones move out of place, or if you alter your garden design and want to change the location of the path, you can pull up the flagstones and reset them. Plus, with sand joints, you can plant between the stones.

That said, there are also good reasons to install a flagstone path over a concrete base and apply mortar between the joints: You

If you plan to use mortar between stones, you'll probably want to make the gaps relatively narrow and uniform. Joints $1/2$ to 1 inch wide look best.

can use thinner stones, down to 1 inch thick, which weigh and cost less. You won't have to fuss over getting plants to root in the cramped spaces between stones, nor are you likely to battle weeds there. The path will also be easier to clean. Besides sweeping or blowing it free of leaves, you can rinse it with a stream of water from a hose or even aim a power sprayer at it to dislodge slippery moss. If you tried this with a dry-laid path, you'd wash away the sand joints.

DEALING WITH DRAINAGE ISSUES

The more solid your path, the more you need to provide good drainage.

- If you live where the ground freezes more than a few inches deep, excavate the path area by at least 12 inches so you can add enough gravel to keep water from puddling directly under the paving. Ice forming there could dislodge the stones. In milder regions, you need to excavate only 7 inches deep.
- Add two layers of fill: $5/8$-inch crushed gravel (with finer particles included), topped by 1 or 2 inches of masonry sand or paver base, also known as stone dust. If drainage is a big problem, use $3/4$- or $1 1/4$-inch gravel without fines for the first layer.
- Slope the path at least $1/8$ inch per foot from one side to the other or one end to the other.

CUTTING FLAGSTONES

It's relatively simple to trim flagstones, either with hand tools or with a power saw or angle grinder fitted with a diamond or abrasive blade. Be sure to wear goggles even for small trimming jobs; if you are using power tools, add ear protection and a respirator that blocks fine dust.

To cut flagstones by hand, you basically chip a notch along the cutting line, then place a straightedge underneath and snap the pieces apart.

You can chisel the line with a brick set and a small sledge-hammer, but the job is far easier if you use tools designed for cutting stone. Stone chisels, such as tracers, have narrower blades and wider shanks, so more force from the hammer meets the stone. A stonecutter's hand hammer, which has a thick, beveled head and a short wooden handle, is perfectly balanced for striking stone chisels.

1 Place the flagstone under its neighbor and mark the cutting line with a pencil.

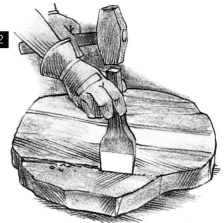

2 Set aside the neighboring stone and score a 1/8-inch-deep groove along the cutting line using a tracer or other stone chisel and a hammer.

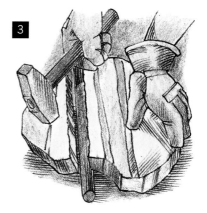

3 Place a metal pipe or an angle iron under the stone so that the waste portion and the scored line overhang it. Strike the waste portion to split the flagstone.

How to Cut with a Circular Saw or Grinder

Instead of scoring the line with a chisel, cut a groove with a circular saw or an angle grinder. Although you can use an abrasive blade with either tool, a diamond blade makes quicker, smoother cuts. Work where the dust won't bother neighbors. Make shallow cuts, lowering the blade 1/8 inch at each pass, until the groove is one-fourth the depth of the stone. Then snap the pieces apart as you would if you were cutting by hand.

To keep down dust, you can dribble water across the stone as you cut—but only if your saw or grinder is labeled as double-insulated. (Using the tool with water may void the warranty, however.) Or set a fan in front of you and a sprinkler behind you so the dust blows into the sprinkler's mist and settles to the ground.

LAYING FLAGSTONES IN A SAND BED

Building a dry-laid flagstone path is an ambitious project, but it's rewarding. One advantage of tackling this type of path rather than one with mortared joints is that you can take your time and even redo individual steps if your first attempt doesn't turn out the way you want. Edging is optional; see page 27 for some possibilities.

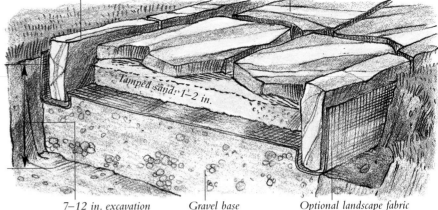

Optional edging (type will vary)

Top surface at least ½ in. above soil; flagstone paving: 1½ in. minimum thickness

Tamped sand: 1–2 in.

7–12 in. excavation

Gravel base (thickness varies)

Optional landscape fabric

1 With garden hoses, extension cords, stakes and string, or spray paint, mark the path's perimeter. Excavate the entire path area. Go down a minimum of 7 inches where winters are mild or 12 inches where the ground freezes more than a few inches deep. If you'll be installing deep edging, such as pavers placed vertically, dig straight down along the edges so the pieces will rest against undisturbed soil. Otherwise, excavate a slightly wider area so you have room to work. Go out 8 inches beyond the perimeter if you are using metal or plastic edging with spikes that must be pounded into gravel.

2 Add 3 inches of gravel, or less if it would get in the way of any edging you are using. Dampen the gravel, then pack it down with a hand tamper or a motorized plate compactor.

3 Add more gravel in layers of 3 inches or less, leaving room at the top for 1 to 2 inches of sand and the flagstones. Dampen and compact each gravel layer before adding the next. Cover the gravel with landscape fabric, if you're using it, and install any edging when the gravel base is at the appropriate height.

Shovel on the sand. (Or substitute paver base, which compacts better because it incorporates particles in a wider size range.) Rake it into a uniform layer that will compress to the thickness you need.

4 Move large stones into the path and position them where they look good and won't need much trimming. Stones with at least one straight side work well along the path's perimeter. Don't worry about leveling them at this point.

Working on a section perhaps 8 feet long, fill in with smaller flagstones. Make any cuts that are necessary. Remove all the flagstones in that section, keeping them in the same order.

5 One at a time, reposition the stones, using a trowel to scrape away or pile up sand until each stone is secure and level with adjacent stones. Remember to provide the slope needed for drainage. To avoid having to reposition big stones, smooth the sand slightly higher than you think it needs to be, then remove a handful from the center of the space before you lower the stone; twist the stone until it's securely set and at the right height. Excess sand will flow into the hole you created under the stone. Check stones frequently with a level to make sure you aren't creating humps or dips. Correct any problems before you proceed.

6 As you finish each section, pack sand into the joints and other small areas with a short length of ⅜-inch rebar; use a scrap of wood to pack straight sections.

7 When all stones are set, sprinkle on more sand or paver base. Sweep or brush it into the crevices and mist the path well. Dribble more along any voids that appear. Keep adding and sweeping until the material no longer disappears from the surface. Only at this point is the path firm enough to walk on.

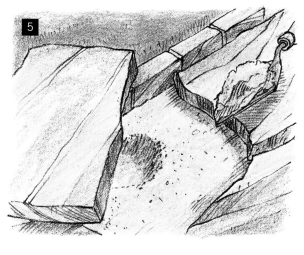

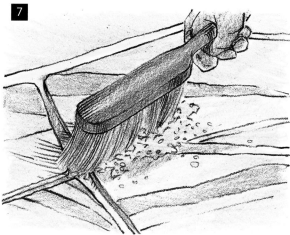

LAYING FLAGSTONES IN WET MORTAR

An old concrete path makes a good base for a mortared flagstone path, if the concrete is clean and in good condition. If you pour a new slab, rough up the hardening concrete with a broom so the mortar will stick better. Let the concrete cure for at least three days before you begin the stonework.

If you are using edging (see page 27), install it before fitting the flagstones. Rest the edging on the concrete, if possible. Trial-fit and trim the flagstones, as you would for a dry-laid path. If the underlying concrete has spaces separating slab sections, keep stones to either side of them to prevent cracks.

When all the stones are in place, remove pieces in a section of about 10 or 12 square feet and set them, in order, to the side. Dampen the concrete and the stones, and blot up any standing water.

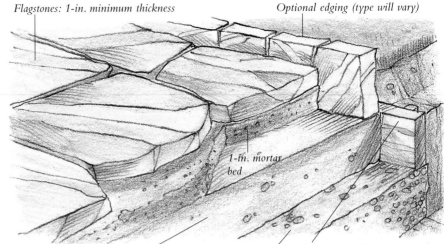

Flagstones: 1-in. minimum thickness   Optional edging (type will vary)

1-in. mortar bed

3½-in. concrete slab   Gravel base: 4–6 in.   Concrete form (leave or remove)

Prepare a bagged mortar mix or a homemade batch of 1 part masonry cement to 3 parts sand, plus just enough water to make a stiff mixture.

1 With a pointed trowel, spread mortar over an area big enough for at least two stones. Make a layer 1 inch thick, or even thicker if the stone for that spot is unusually thin. Think of the mortar as a leveling device. Furrow the mortar with the trowel.

2 Lower one stone onto the mortar. Bed the stone by tapping it with a rubber mallet, but don't force the mortar to gush up around the stone. Lower the next stone and tap it with the mallet to line up this piece with the first stone. Continue in this way, working your way across the path and then forward. As you proceed, check the surface with a level to make sure the stones meet evenly and the overall surface slants at least ⅛ inch per foot sideways or lengthwise for drainage. Clean

The Best of Both Worlds

With a bit of cleverness, you can build a flagstone path with sand joints and yet wind up with most of the benefits of mortared joints.

Build a dry-laid path, but instead of packing sand into the joints as you complete each section, wait until all the stones are in place. Then spread dry mortar mix or dry sand mix (a 1:3 mixture of Portland cement and sand) into the gaps between stones. Use a funnel to channel the mixture into place without getting it all over the stones. Brush any spills off the stones and into the crevices.

Mist with water, using a spray so fine it doesn't wash the mixture out of the joints. Wipe off any splashes with a damp sponge. Keep the path damp for the rest of the day. If a white haze clouds the stones after the path has dried, use a stone cleaner (not a straight muriatic acid wash) to remove the remaining mortar residue.

Because this type of path lacks a concrete base, the joints aren't as frost resistant or strong. You will likely need to make annual repairs if you live where the ground freezes. The joints probably won't stand up to pressure-washing either.

up any mortar spills on the stones with a damp sponge.

3 Let the mortar set 24 hours, then grout the joints with a fresh batch of mortar. Apply it with a mortar bag, which is like an oversize cake-decorating bag, or with a trowel. Aim to make the mortar flush with the surface of the stone. Do not attempt to smooth the mortar immediately or you'll make a mess.

4 Shape the mortar when it stiffens a bit, or "bones up." With your trowel, press down on the grout to force it into any hidden crevices. Then shape the top surface as you wish. With the trowel, you can smooth the grout flat or push it down to make V-shaped valleys. Or use a wire loop (homemade or purchased from a masonry supply store) to cut a slightly rounded indentation. Whichever method you choose, cut off the excess grout and lift it away with a trowel; don't smear it around on the stones. Clean the stones with a damp sponge as you go.

Keep the grout damp for at least three days by misting the path with water and covering it with plastic. After that, you can use the path.

Tight-fitting, natural-looking joints are hallmarks of fine craftsmanship in a flagstone path set in wet mortar.

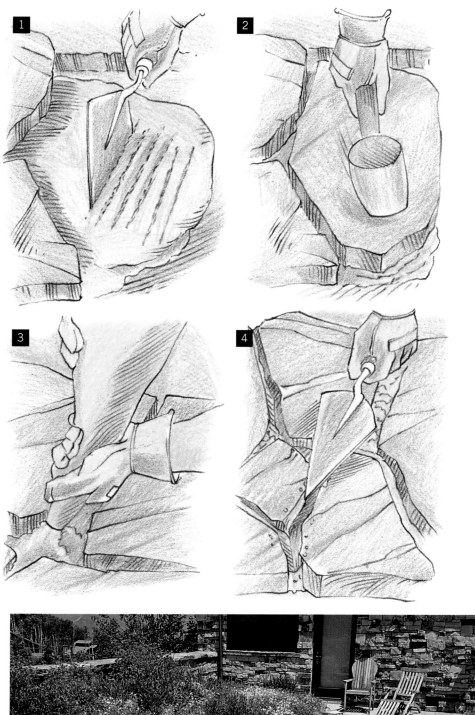

PLANTING IN AND ALONG A FLAGSTONE PATH

Gaps between flagstones in a dry-laid path hardly qualify as prime real estate for most plants. But some varieties do thrive in these cramped, desertlike spaces, and they are not all weeds. Consider the following plants, all of which stay low to the ground. Along the edges of a path, you may also want to consider the somewhat taller plants suggested for use around stepping-stones (see pages 20–21).

To plant, excavate small sections of sand between stones with a tiny trowel or a screwdriver. Tuck in small plants and backfill with good potting soil. Or plant along the path's edges and count on the plants to worm their way into spaces between stones.

Dichondra

Hardy to 13°F/–11°C. Sun or partial shade. Regular water. Moderate foot traffic. Grows 2–6 inches tall with leaves like tiny lily pads. *D. argentea,* native to Texas and Mexico, is heat and drought tolerant.

Green carpet

On partially shady paths, dwarf mondo grass performs better between stones than lawn grass does. Unlike lawn, dwarf mondo grass stays neat without mowing.

Green carpet or rupture wort

Herniaria glabra / Hardy to –20°F/–29°C. Sun or shade. Regular water. Occasional foot traffic. Trailing plant has tiny, bright green leaves less than ¼ inch long. Leaves turn bronzy red in winter. Needs good drainage.

Irish or Scotch moss

Sagina subulata / Hardy in all climates. Full sun or part shade. Regular water. Some foot traffic. Forms a dense, moss-like carpet between paving stones. Green forms are called Irish moss; golden green forms, Scotch moss. Tiny white flowers bloom in spring. Needs good soil and drainage.

Jewel mint of Corsica

Mentha requienii / Hardy to –10°F/ –12°C. Sun or part shade. Regular water. Some foot traffic. Forms a creeping, bright green mat that looks similar to moss, but with tiny purple flowers in summer. Leaves release a minty or sagelike fragrance when stepped on. Can be invasive.

Mazus reptans

Mazus reptans

Hardy to –40°F/–40°C. Sun, but part shade in hot areas. Regular water. Heavy foot traffic. Creeps and roots, creating a mat about 2 inches tall. Flowers resemble snapdragons. Dies back in cold winters but usually regrows. Can spread into nearby lawn.

Mondo grass

Ophiopogon japonicus / Hardy to 10°F/–12°C. Partial shade best. Regular to moderate water. Occasional foot traffic. Dwarf forms, such as 'Kyoto Dwarf' and 'Nana', create grasslike carpet 3–4 inches tall; lilac flowers are mostly hidden by leaves. Evergreen, but yellows after several freezes.

Sandwort

Arenaria / Hardiness varies. Water needs vary. Moderate foot traffic. Forms a dense mat that resembles moss, but has small white flowers. Can be invasive. Corsican sandwort *(A. balearica)* does well in shade, while mountain sandwort *(A. montana)* thrives in sun.

Sandwort

Ground Cover Thymes

Hardy and fragrant when stepped on, thyme is the quintessential companion for flagstones. But how to choose from among the many types?

- Look at the general shape of the plants at the nursery. Even in small pots, trailing types grow horizontally more than upright types do, which is what you want between flagstones. Plan on clipping the plants back periodically so they don't get too leggy.

- To evaluate a thyme's tendency to become leggy quickly, examine the length of stem that shows between clusters of leaves. Plants with closely spaced leaf clusters grow slowly and are likely to remain compact longer. They're best for narrow spaces.

- Consider leaf color and how it contrasts with your stepping-stones. Thyme leaves can be silver, chartreuse, green, gold, or reddish. Flowers range from white to dark pink, but they last for only a short time, so leaf color matters most.

- Do you want bees? If not, choose a nonflowering species such as woolly thyme *(Thymus pseudolanuginosus).*

fieldstone paths

Literally meaning stone found in a field, fieldstone can encompass almost any rock that wasn't recently blasted free in a quarry or tumbled round on a beach.

Because it's been out in the weather for years, fieldstone is often beautifully flecked with patches of moss or lichen. These touches may seem meaningless in a pathway, where footsteps can wear away lichen and where moss can cause people to slip, but the fact that fieldstone exists means you can select some as garden accents and install paving that matches.

Fieldstone is one of the best types of rock to use if you want to create a timeless or antique look in your garden.

ABOVE: *When a path winds through persistent shade, slippery moss can begin to coat the surface. The rough texture of fieldstones adds a measure of safety.*

LEFT: *Because fieldstone is available in a wide array of sizes and shapes, it's easy to create paths and walls that match. On this gentle slope, large stones create steps while smaller stones fill in behind. Careful fitting results in a relatively smooth surface that's suitable even for busy pathways.*

INSET: *Adorned with lichen, a fieldstone path marches single-file through a planting bed. A path like this should be used only occasionally because heavy traffic would wear away the lichen.*

LEFT: *To widen narrow field-stone paths and make them easier to use, fill gaps with fairly chunky gravel and small stones, as shown in both these paths. If you cut the field-stones to fit, this is a good way to use up the waste pieces.*

DESIGNING A FIELDSTONE PATH

If you're working with stone that's already on your property, first take stock of what you have. You might want to sort the usable stone into a pile to help you estimate what area you can cover. Overall size doesn't matter; count just the face you'll point up. In most cases, that will be the largest flat face.

If you have enough large stones, you may want to use them on the edges of your path and fill the middle with smaller stones. Even such a relatively informal pattern lends beauty and order to a path. Or, if you have a few extremely large stones and many small ones, you can position the large ones in key spots and build most of the path around them.

Design Tip

Fieldstone paving generally looks rather rustic. If you want a more polished look, establish a pattern. For example, place large pieces along edges of your path and fill in between with smaller stones.

BUYING FIELDSTONE

Although you can build a path from stones with only one flat face, custom-digging each hole is a lot of work. If you are buying fieldstone, look for pieces with two relatively flat faces. If these stones tend to be almost the same thickness, that's even better.

Count a surface as flat even if it has a few high spots poking out. You can easily knock these off as you build. But avoid using a dish-shaped surface. If you run short and need to use one, chisel a little channel so water and ice won't collect.

LEFT: *Framed beautifully by an open gate, this fieldstone path carries the eye off into the distance and makes the garden seem larger than it is.*

BELOW: *Because fieldstone paths are relatively rough, they encourage visitors to slow down and enjoy a garden or natural area. To underscore this idea, provide seating at a key spot or two.*

"Free" Fieldstone

It goes without saying that you should never help yourself to stone on property other than your own without asking. However, there are many situations where people may be happy to give permission. Where the ground freezes deep, farmers often have to clear their fields of stone each spring. They may be only too happy to let you help. You might also inquire where new development is under way.

National parks are off-limits, of course. But if you live near a national forest, you may be able to get a permit to gather landscaping stone there. Call a nearby ranger station, listed under U.S. Forest Service in the government section of the telephone book.

If you do gather stone on your own, you'll probably want to transport it in the back of a pickup truck. Even then, do not attempt to carry too heavy a load, especially over bumpy forest roads.

BUILDING A FIELDSTONE PATH

You can build a fieldstone path like a series of stepping-stones, setting each stone individually, or fit the stones together like flagstones on a gravel base prepared ahead of time. The best approach depends on how much the stones vary in thickness and size, as well as on how big a project you want to tackle at once.

THE STEPPING-STONE METHOD To build a fieldstone path as if it were a collection of stepping-stones, you simply excavate for each stone, set it, and then proceed to the next stone. If you are building with stones that you haul home a few at a time, this is the way to go because it doesn't make much of a mess. You also generate far less surplus dirt, and you avoid buying large quantities of gravel. Also, the path can evolve in a free-form way, taking advantage of the particular stones that you find.

To make it easier to level the stones, dig slightly oversize holes and add sand to the bottom so that you can make fine adjustments to the stones' placement in this looser material. When you're satisfied with a stone's alignment, pack sand into any gaps, water gently, and wait for the moisture to drain away (perhaps overnight). Then add more sand to fill gaps. Repeat until all gaps are filled. Don't step on the stone until then.

THE FLAGSTONE METHOD If the area you need to cover is large, you may prefer to excavate soil for a gravel bed and lay the fieldstones on top rather than dig individual holes—especially if the stones are small or relatively flat and about equally thick. The process is much like that for dry-laying flagstones on pages 46–47. But there are a few differences to accommodate the greater variation in the thickness of the stones.

A mixture of fieldstones and flagstones gives texture to the paving in this herb garden. Note how the central circle, the focus of attention, is several stones wide in places, while a secondary path used mostly for tending the planting beds consists of fieldstones set as stepping-stones.

For a wide fieldstone path like this, consider digging out the entire route and adding gravel fill so you can simply set the pieces on top, rather than excavating for each one.

position just once, particularly if the stone is large. This means you should make any major cuts beforehand. Use newspaper or cardboard patterns if it's hard to visualize and remember the shapes you are trying to create. Also measure each new stone's thickness and compare it with the thickness of surrounding stones you have already placed. This will help you determine how much gravel to add or remove before you lower the new stone into place. To fine-tune the height and orientation of a stone once it is in the gravel, use a pry bar or the wide blade of a mattock to raise an edge of the stone and a trowel to add or remove gravel underneath.

- Determine how deep to excavate by measuring the thickest stones and adding 2 inches. (If a couple of stones are unusually thick, don't include them in this calculation; you can always dig deeper just for those stones.)
- Plan for the gravel to nearly fill the hole, leaving just enough space at the top for the average-thickness stones. Do not add a layer of paver base or masonry sand on top of the gravel fill.
- Instead of arranging all the stones and then removing them so they can be permanently seated one by one, as you would with flagstones, try to lower each fieldstone into

- Once a stone is in position, if you see that a small protrusion prevents a good fit, nudge the stone a few inches away from its neighbor and make the cut there.

HOW TO SHAPE FIELDSTONES

Shape fieldstone with the same methods you'd use for flagstones (see page 45), but try these techniques if you need to change the shape only slightly (be sure to wear goggles as you work):

- To remove a small high spot, chisel at different angles around the bulge until it pops free. If your chisel skids across the surface, strike straight down near the bulge to cut a divot where you can rest the chisel tip as you make the angle cut.

- To remove a large bump, cut parallel lines into it with a circular saw or grinder, then chisel off the little walls of stone that remain between the cuts. Or break away the bump little by little, using a mason's hand hammer and chisel, or a mash hammer, which is designed for striking stone directly.

cut stone paths

Cut stone can look prim and proper or be almost playful, depending on how you arrange the pieces. Large slabs of bluestone set into a grid of vertical and horizontal lines create a gracious look suitable for even the most formal entries and entertaining areas, while a harlequin pattern of contrasting stones conveys a hipper mood. Whatever the style, the flat, regular surface provides safe, welcoming paving even in the most demanding locations.

Set with plenty of gaps for plants, the stone path on the facing page helps frame the view of an ornate wall adorned with tile. The path below, with its closely spaced stones, is more suitable for heavy traffic. The irregular arrangement still allows greenery in the path.

ABOVE: *It's relatively easy to incorporate angles, circles or other shapes in cut stone paving. Two grids, one set at a 45-degree angle from the other, result in an intriguing combination of bluestone pavers and granite cobblestones (top), while a circular design (bottom) creates an opportunity for a path to widen into a sitting area with a small herb garden. This design would also work as paving where a path meets a birdbath, flagpole, or other garden ornament.*

DESIGNING A CUT STONE PATH

With a cut stone path, the type of rock, the shape and size of the pieces, and the way they are set all affect the final result.

If you have a Colonial or other traditional-looking house, bluestone may look best because it has long been used for paving in the East, where the Colonial style evolved. If you have an adobe-style house, however, paving cut from Arizona sandstone might be a better fit.

For a formal look, use relatively smooth stones set in a precise geometric pattern. Mortar the joints, or butt pieces tightly together. For a more relaxed look, combine stones of different sizes, shapes, or colors, or select pieces with more texture. Instead of setting the stones in a precise pattern, you might try an arrangement that has a sense of order but avoids being too predictable, perhaps with large stones where your foot lands with every other step and

clusters of smaller stones in the remaining spots.

Cut stone paths can be laid in wet mortar over concrete or in sand or dry mortar over gravel and sand, just as with flagstones. Mortared paths are easiest to keep clean and might be the best option by the main entry to your house. Also, placing the stone on concrete is the obvious choice if you have an existing concrete path that you want to dress up. With sand joints, you have the option of encouraging

low, tough plants to grow between stones.

Unless cut stone pieces are unusually big and thick, plan to use edging (see page 27) if you set stones in sand or dry mortar; edging is optional if the pieces are more than about 20 inches square and 2 inches thick, or if you set the stones on a concrete base with wet mortar.

LEFT: *A few especially large pieces make a path seem luxuriously wide, even though some of the stones are relatively small.*

ABOVE: *Flat stones frame a single flagstone with a cleaved surface, focusing attention on its natural look (top). Stone pavers of different colors create a multicolored quilt pattern that fits with the Southwest style of this garden (bottom). Placing the stones with their longest dimension in line with the path, rather than across it as is more commonly done, makes the path seem longer than it is.*

BUYING CUT STONE

From tile-size squares of red sandstone to sidewalk-size slabs of slate or bluestone, you'll find much to choose from when you shop for cut stone. Besides looking at stone yards and garden centers, you may want to investigate home centers and tile stores. Some of what you find won't work for exterior paving because it's too slippery, but you should still find plenty of suitable stone.

Cut stone, by definition, always has sawn edges and a flat back. But the top can be left natural or textured in a variety of ways. Some of your choices in surfaces:

NATURAL, SPLIT, OR CLEAVED A slightly undulating surface that results when stone is split along a natural seam.

HONED A smooth but matte finish created by grinding the surface with a coarse abrasive. Honed stone usually has enough traction to be used outdoors, but if the stone is glossy or reflective it qualifies as polished and is too slick for paths.

FLAMED, OR THERMAL A rough but uniform surface created when the stone is exposed to a torch. The intense heat causes crystals in the stone to shatter, producing the texture.

TUMBLED A distressed finish that results when stone is tossed into what's essentially a giant cement mixer. The sharp edges wear off and the stone emerges with a softer, slightly antique look.

BUSH HAMMERED A pitted or grooved texture applied with a pneumatic tool that pounds the stone.

PICKED Stone that's cut to size and then made to look more rustic by roughening it with a hand pick. Picked stone is often used as edging.

SAND BLASTED A slightly rough surface with a matte finish created with a high-pressure blast of sand and water.

SAWN A smooth or slightly ridged surface created by a saw cut. Ridges can be either straight or circular, depending on the blade used.

Buy stone at least 1½ inches thick if you plan to install it on a bed of gravel and sand and use sand or dry mortar in the joints. Thicker stone is even better, particularly if pieces are small. Over concrete, stone 1 to 1½ inches works well. Thinner cut stone pieces aren't suitable for outdoor paving, even with mortar.

With some types of cut stone, the thickness is virtually uniform from piece to piece. With others, there may be considerable variation. The lack of uniformity can make installation more difficult if you want a perfectly level surface, but if you want added texture, it becomes an asset.

The dimensions listed for cut stone may be either the actual length and width or "nominal" dimensions, which are bigger than the stone because they include an allowance for mortar joints of a specific thickness. Be sure to ask about this when you calculate how much to buy.

Picked granite

Bush hammered granite

Sand blasted sandstone

Natural split basalt

Tumbled travertine

Sawn China green slate

Sawn, tumbled marble

Flamed granite

ABOVE: *A variety of colors adds vitality to this stone path. The golden-colored pieces were interspersed along the route, and the pavers were laid in a basketweave pattern.*

RIGHT: *Lush, green baby's tears creeps between paving stones, making their rosy color seem more vivid. If you want to plant within a cut stone path, buy stones at least 1½ inches thick so you can install them on a plant-friendly base of gravel and sand. Thinner stone must be set on concrete.*

LAYING OUT A CUT STONE PATH

Since cut stone comes in a specific geometric shape, you will save a lot of work by building your design around the shape you select. Make the path's width a multiple of the stone's width, so you don't have to cut every edge piece.

Begin the design phase with an exploratory shopping trip to determine what kind of stone you like and what sizes are available. Before you buy anything, play with possible patterns by sketching on graph paper. Use a scale of at least ½ inch to the foot so that you have enough room to draw in the stones. You can also cut out small pieces of paper to represent stones and move them around to test different patterns.

Even with the simplest of stone shapes—squares of a single size—you have more options than you might think. You can arrange these stones in even rows, in staggered rows, or on a diagonal. If the stones are rectangular, you can try all those designs and then go on to basketweave and herringbone patterns. You can create even more intricate designs if you use stones of several sizes.

DECIDING ON EDGING

Edging is optional for mortared paths laid over concrete, but if you choose to use it, rest the edging on the concrete before fitting the stones, or wedge it between the slab and the soil. If you're using heavy cut stone— such as slabs of bluestone 2 inches thick and 2 feet square—in sand or dry mortar, you don't need edging either because the pieces are heavy enough that they'll stay put. But if you're using 1½-inch-thick pieces only

ABOVE: *A path of large, interlocking cut stone pavers under a rose arbor is reminiscent of a walkway in an English manor garden.*

LEFT: *Cut stone comes in a variety of sizes, so you can work out interesting designs that don't require you to cut any pieces. Go with an irregular edge, if you wish.*

12 inches square, you need edging to keep the stones from shifting. With sizes in between, you can decide based on the stability of your soil, how much traffic you expect the path to get, and how much it matters whether all the stones stay perfectly aligned.

Deep edging, such as vertical pieces of cut stone or bricks on end, should be installed against undisturbed soil, so make straight up-and-down cuts when you dig the edges of the excavation. Spread gravel underneath if you need to raise these pieces to the height you want.

Plastic edging made for use with concrete pavers is especially easy to use with cut stone, since concrete pavers and cut sone have similar dimensions and shapes. Look for this edging at masonry supply stores. With this style, you'll need to extend the excavated area 8 inches beyond the perimeter of the path. Add and compact the gravel, then install the edging along the perimeter lines. Drive landscape spikes through it into the gravel base. The edging will form a dam to hold in a layer of sand and the stones. (For more on installing edging, see page 27.)

RIGHT: *As you design your stone path, think about not just the pattern of the stones, but also how plants along the edges will affect the overall look. Here, English ivy and lady's-mantle soften what otherwise might seem a monotonous stretch of identical square pavers.*

INSTALLING CUT STONE ON A SAND BASE

Installing cut stone on a base of sand and gravel is similar to working with flagstones (see pages 46–47). But you can incorporate several time-saving steps that take advantage of the stones' uniform shape and thickness. If you space the stones close together, you also need to pay more attention to drainage (see pages 44 and 79).

1 Lay out the perimeter of the path using stakes and string. If you use stones with right angles, ensure 90-degree angles in your layout wherever possible. At each corner, measure out 3 feet along one side and 4 feet along the other. Adjust the strings until the end points are exactly 5 feet apart. When all stakes are in place, mark one at the eventual height of the paving, then measure up by a distance that clears grass or other landscaping. Make another mark there. With string

and a line level, transfer this height to the other stakes. Mark stakes on the downward side to account for a slope of $\frac{1}{8}$ to $\frac{1}{4}$ inch per foot.

2 Excavate at least 7 inches where winters are mild or 12 inches where the ground freezes. If you are not using edging or are using a deep type, such as cut stone set vertically, excavate just to the edge of the path. If you are using metal or plastic edging pinned with stakes, go out 8 inches beyond the path's perimeter.

3 Install the gravel base and add edging, if you are using it, when the gravel is at the appropriate height. If you skip edging, install 2-by-4 temporary edge forms as if they were permanent wooden edging. Add the gravel in layers no more than 3 inches deep. After each addition, dampen the gravel with water and compact the stones with a hand tamper or a motorized plate compactor. Go over all areas several times before you add more gravel. Stop adding gravel when there's just enough room for the sand and stones.

Temporary or permanent edging

Stone paving: 1½-in. minimum thickness; top surface at least ½ in. above soil

Sand: 1–2 in.

Base of ⅝-in. gravel (depth varies)

Optional extra gravel for poorly drained sites

Optional landscape fabric

7–12 in. or more

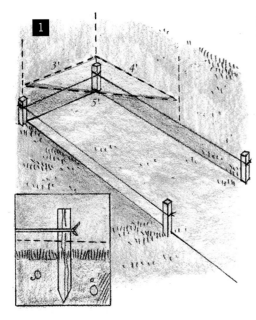

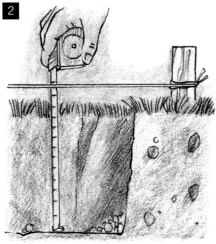

4 Add the sand (or substitute paver base, a mixture of stone dust and shards) and roughly level it with a rake. Tamp. Take out high spots and find low spots to fill by running a screed along the edging or temporary edge forms. When the sand is level, compact it a final time and saturate it with a fine mist of water. Wait, probably overnight, for it to drain completely. Run the screed along the path a final time and level any uneven spots.

5 Aim to create equal-size joints, usually about ½ inch wide, but don't worry if you need to fudge by ⅛ inch or so to accommodate differences in the stones. Use a mallet to seat each stone, then check its alignment with a level. If you need to move a stone, try to scoot it on trowel blades rather than slide it on the sand, so you don't dig ruts into the base. If your design calls for vertical or horizontal joints to line up, stop every few rows and check your progress.

6 After you have set all the full stones, cut and install the partial pieces. Fill joints with sand or paver base. Do this by tossing the sand over the stones and sweeping it into the joints. Spray the path lightly with water and repeat until no more sand goes into the joints.

Trimming Cut Stone

You can trim cut stone by the same methods you'd use for flagstones, but if your pieces aren't too big, there are easier options. First, consider renting a tile saw or a brick saw. The main limitation is the size piece that the saw can cut. Brick saws generally have a larger capacity than tile saws. Wear goggles and ear protectors when using these tools. Or ask whether the stone yard or store where you shopped will make the cuts for you.

INSTALLING CUT STONE ON CONCRETE

The procedure is the same as for flagstones (shown in step 4), but because cut stone is more uniform, it's easier to set. Nail 1-inch spacer boards to the top of the concrete forms, if they are still in place, or install temporary edge forms so that you can screed the mortar into a level layer (as you would do in step 4 for cut stones on a sand base). Be sure joints between stones line up with any control joints in the concrete or the stones will eventually crack.

cobblestones

For creating a path with an antique look, nothing beats cobblestones, also known as Belgian blocks. These cut stones are small but especially thick, with sawn sides and rough, natural tops. Some are cubes, generally 4 or 5 inches on each side. Others are shaped more like jumbo bricks, 8 to 12 inches long and maybe 4 or 5 inches wide and thick. The thickness helps cobblestones wedge together and virtually eliminates the risk of splitting.

The added thickness also means you pay for a lot of stone you'll never see once the paving is in place. If you're building a path that will have only light foot traffic, you can create a similar look for less cost by using granite pavers about the size of bricks. With either standard cobblestones or the pavers, you don't need much strength to move individual pieces. A 4-inch granite cube weighs less than 5½ pounds.

If you shop for cobblestones, you'll see mostly freshly cut pieces. You may also find tumbled cobblestones, with rounded edges. A few companies deal in antique cobblestones salvaged from old roads.

INSTALLING COBBLESTONES

Install cobblestones much as you would place other cut stone on a base of gravel and sand. But make these modifications:

- Always use edging. Cobblestone itself works well as edging if you stand brick-shape pieces vertically.
- Don't leave wide gaps between the cobblestones. Instead, butt pieces tightly and fill the crevices with sand.

Cobblestones also make great edging for gravel paths, a point to keep in mind if you want a cobblestone path close to your house and something less formal farther away.

Cobblestones round a curved planting area (below left). Because they're relatively small, they rarely require cutting to fit within the borders of a path. Cobblestones just as easily march down a straight path (below right).

*Although cobble-
stones come in just
two shapes—square
and rectangular—
it's still possible to
create a wide array
of paving designs
with them.*

*Besides paving entire areas, cobblestones can also edge other paving and create decorative designs.
In this path, granite cobblestones create an unusual pathway and garden focus.*

mixed materials

Paths of mixed materials catch the eye and invite people to take delight in contrasting colors and textures. The contrasts can be bold and bright or quite subtle, depending on your style. Either way, this type of paving will help define your garden as a personal space that reflects your creativity. Selecting materials with colors or textures that are similar usually helps create a restful look, while pairing materials with opposite textures or colors results in a livelier path.

Paths of mixed materials benefit from having a unifying organizing principal. For the path on the facing page, elevated edging establishes a symmetrical shape. Filled in with loosely fitted paving, the path has an informal ambiance but still fits with the classically detailed house. In the path below, flagstone pavers define the edges, almost as if the stones were boulders along a streambed.

ABOVE: *Brick, recycled concrete, and round river rocks create an interesting path alongside a house (top). Wooden beams and gravel team up in a path that curves around planting beds (bottom).*

DESIGNING A PATH OF MIXED MATERIALS

A few tricks help keep a path of mixed materials from looking like a jumble of disconnected parts. Just as with plants in a perennial border, the elements of a mixed-materials path look better when they are grouped or repeated, not used singly. If you arrange materials in a pattern, repeat it in some way all along the path. For example, you can lay out a geometric pattern and fill some spaces with one type of paving material and the remaining spaces with another type. Or you can build most of the path with one variety of stone, such as square bluestone pavers, and then tuck in a very different selection, maybe granite cobblestones, wherever the path bends or widens. You can also add contrasting color at regular intervals.

To create the look of a dry stream bed (right), round river rocks were tucked between slabs of flat stone. Below, a few large flagstones set into the cobblestones smooth the transition between different paving materials.

ABOVE: *Small stones can be used effectively to set off larger paving pieces. The path at the top was laid out in a standard brick pattern, but some of the spaces were filled with small rounded stones. In the lower path, gravel unites the cut stone edging and the flagstone pieces in the main traffic lane.*

stone patios

From a construction standpoint, a stone patio is essentially just an extra-wide path. But in how they're used, the two are almost opposites. A path takes you somewhere. At a patio, you've arrived.

Whether you want a place to sit and enjoy a view, to watch birds while you have your morning coffee, or to dine outdoors in the evening, you can choose a location for your patio that will make it a pleasant place to linger. Stone patios aren't generally attached to a house, so you have more leeway in choosing the location than you do with a deck.

BELOW: *To pave a poolside patio, mortared flagstone is a good choice because it can be swept clean or even hosed off. And using mortar between joints reduces the chance that grit will get into the water.*

ABOVE: *This patio also features mortared stone, but the overall look is more rustic because the stones have more texture. Boulders on the edges add to this effect. The large stones on the left act as edging for a planting bed, while the ones on the right serve as steps to a lower garden.*

RIGHT: *A stone terrace can engage all the senses. This one is situated in a sunny spot with a great view. Creeping thyme, planted in spaces between the cut stone pavers, releases its fragrance when stepped on.*

ABOVE: *When you design a stone patio, consider the type of furniture you might place on it. Slender metal legs do fine on a cut stone patio with tight joints (top). Thick wooden pieces are needed on a rough-textured fieldstone patio (bottom).*

DESIGNING A STONE PATIO

While it's possible to build a stone patio on any relatively flat patch of your property, you're more likely to use space that's within sight of the house. If you plan to dine or entertain guests on the patio, consider the distance to the kitchen. Also try to pick a spot that's out of the wind and has the best mix of sunshine and shade for your climate, at least in the hours you'll use the patio. Consider views, too.

Patios often look best when their design cues come from the house, especially if it is nearby. Look at your house from where the patio will be. Search for a dimension that recurs or dominates, such as the distance between porch posts or the width of a wing. Try to echo that dimension or a multiple of it in the patio's design. You may want to line up the patio so it's square with the house; if not, deviate from 90 degrees in some purposeful way. For example, you can set the patio at a 45-degree angle to the back wall.

A patio doesn't have to be enormous, but if you want a dining table there, make the space roomy enough so people can pull out chairs before they sit down. Indoors, the general rule is to allow 2 to 3 feet on all sides of a table as a bare minimum. But outdoor furniture tends to be bigger, so leave 4½ feet if possible.

If you want to cook outdoors, consider including an outdoor kitchen in your design. Lay whatever pipes you need for gas, electricity, or plumbing before you install the gravel base for your patio.

If you live in an area where outdoor fires are allowed, a fire ring may be a wonderful addition to your patio.

Trellises and arbors make large patios more inviting. Besides helping to define seating or dining areas, they provide supports for shady vines, awnings, or even standard roofing.

To create a cozy dining area, build a patio that seems more like a wide spot in a path, rather than a large expanse of pavement. Sand joints and textured stone enhance this look, as do lush planting beds along the edges.

Outdoor spaces benefit from some of the same tricks that interior decorators use to make indoor areas more cozy. On this patio, a stepped-down area paved with small stones provides a comfortable sitting area near the fire.

DECIDING ON STONE TYPE

Any type of stone you can use for a path can be used for a patio. Consider these points when choosing:

- If you plan to have furniture on the patio, consider how even the surface needs to be. If you have delicate metal chairs with tiny feet, you may need to use large cut stone pieces with joints that are either very narrow or filled with mortar. But if you have wooden furniture with thick legs, irregular flagstone with sand joints may be fine—especially if you put large flagstones where chairs will be pulled in and out.

- If you expect crowds of kids to use the patio for art projects, slurping ice cream, and other messy activities, consider a gravel patio. Spills usually disappear on gravel, without any effort on your part. But keep this type of patio some distance from your house so the gravel doesn't get tracked in.

- Cut stone is perfect for a square, rectangular, or other strongly geometric patio. But if you want your patio to have a meandering shape, flagstone or fieldstone may look better because their shape meanders a bit, too. Gravel adapts to anything.

Design Tip

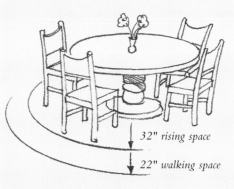

32" *rising space*

22" *walking space*

Allow 4½ feet of clearance all around the dining table. The more room there is, the more gracious the space will feel.

BUILDING A STONE PATIO

Once you decide on a type of stone, you can build a patio using the same basic steps that you'd use for a path. The layout steps are slightly different, however, and provisions for drainage are more important. These directions are for a rectangular patio that runs lengthwise along the back of a house, but you can adapt them for other situations.

1 Drive stakes into the ground and tie on string to mark the area you need to excavate. Keep the stakes back a bit, as shown, so they aren't in your way as you dig and build the patio. If you are using edging that will be held in place with stakes, the string should be at least 8 inches beyond the eventual edges of the patio. Otherwise, adjust the dimensions for the type of edging you are using (see page 27). To be sure the corners are all right angles, measure the distance between each stake next to the house and the corner diagonally across from it. The two distances should be equal.

2 Use a builder's level, which stands on tripod legs, to help you mark the eventual height of the patio on the stakes. Be sure to measure up far enough to clear lawn or other vegetation. Or mark the patio height on one stake next to the house. Tie a string to that spot. Stretch the string to the stake straight out from the house and tie a knot. Slip on a line level (a small tool that hooks over the string) and raise or lower the second knot until the string is level. Mark that height and repeat the process until you have marked all stakes.

3 Divide the distance the patio extends out from the house, in feet, by 8. The result is the number of inches the patio must slope away from the house to ensure that rainwater will drain. On the outer stakes, measure down by this amount from the first marks you made. This is the finished elevation, plus the gap you left to clear vegetation.

4 Using these reference points, excavate soil, add base materials, and install edging, as you would for a path. If it's a large area, you might need additional reference lines. Just add more stakes and string every 5 feet or so.

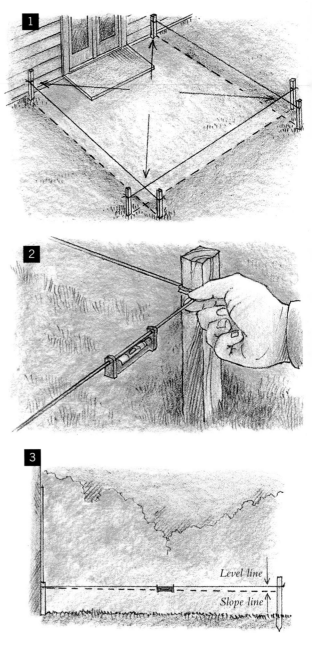

Level line

Slope line

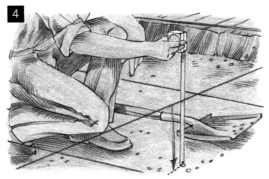

DEALING WITH DRAINAGE

If you are planning a large patio or have soil that drains poorly, you may need to provide an easy way for water to flow safely away. Dig a trench about 12 inches deep (deeper if the ground freezes) on the down-ward edge of the patio and line it with filter cloth. Then add perforated pipe, with the holes pointed down so gravel won't plug them. If your property slopes, extend the trench and add unperforated pipe to carry the water downhill to a point

Even stone patios with sand or plants between joints need an adequate drainage plan because the relatively large percentage of stone keeps the soil from absorbing water as quickly as it normally could.

where it can flow out and not be a problem. If your land is flat, extend the pipe instead to a gravel-filled pit away from all structures.

Before you cover up the pipe, check with a level to make sure all sections slant downhill. Then fill around perforated sections with round, washed gravel. Cover solid sections of pipe with soil.

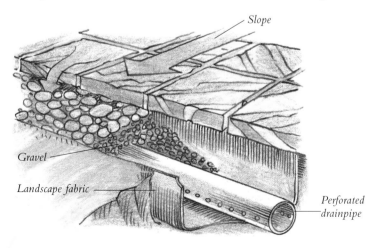

Slope

Gravel

Landscape fabric

Perforated drainpipe

steps and staircases

In some yards, stairs are an essential part of every coming and going. But even if you have a lot that barely slopes, you might want a step or two simply as a decorative flourish, a way to add a bit of drama, or to separate sections of your garden. Stone steps can also give you a place to sit and chat with a neighbor or to spread out a newspaper and read in the sunshine. And if you have creative kids, you may want to add stone steps simply because they serve as props for countless adventures. As you plan your steps, also begin thinking about what kind of plants you will add next to them. Besides adding beauty, plants help prevent erosion. Use sprawling plants, or at least include some of them in your design. If you plant only varieties that grow straight up, you'll be looking at a lot of bare dirt as you climb the steps. Sprawlers look good whether you're coming or going.

Stone steps can take many forms. If you have slabs that are big enough, you can build each step from a single piece or even chip two steps from one stone (facing page). Granite blocks (top right) form the riser and leading edge of steps where the treads are mostly lawn. With careful fitting and a little mortar, relatively small stones make a pleasant staircase (right). And a ribbon of water adds drama to cut stone steps that have ledgestone risers (below).

DESIGNING STEPS AND STAIRCASES

The reason some steps are pleasant to climb while others seem awkward probably stems from their proportions. This handy formula sums up what works: the depth of the treads plus twice the rise should equal 25 to 27 inches.

For outdoor steps, a rise of 4 to 6½ inches ensures an easy climb, while a rise between 5 and 7 inches gets people up and down quickly but still safely. Stair treads should be at least 13 inches deep. The ideal combination, according to some landscape architects, is 15-inch treads with a 6-inch rise.

DETERMINING RISE AND RUN
Begin by measuring the rise (the height difference from the top of the slope to the bottom) and the run (its horizontal length).

With a helper, place a long, straight board so it hangs out horizontally from the top of the slope. When the board is level, measure its height at the bottom of the slope. This is the rise.

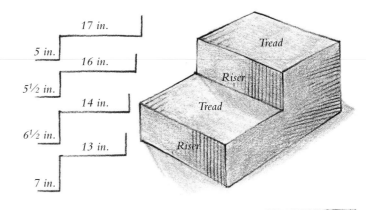

17 in.
5 in.
16 in.
5½ in.
14 in.
6½ in.
13 in.
7 in.

Tread
Riser
Tread
Riser

6-in. riser
15-in. tread

The run is the horizontal distance back to the top of the slope. Measure a long slope in sections; add the results to get the total rise and the total run. Drive stakes where you want the steps to begin and end. String twine between them. Attach a line level and move the string until it's level. Then measure down for the rise and back to the first stake for the run.

CALCULATING STEP DIMENSIONS
To determine how many steps you need and their dimensions, decide what riser height you'd like. Divide that into the total rise (in inches). Round off the fraction and you'll have the number of steps you need.

Then divide the number of steps into the total rise. The answer is the exact riser height you need, if the bottom step starts at ground level and you provide a landing stone or paving at the top of the slope that matches the thickness of the treads. If not, subtract the thickness of one tread from the total rise before you make the calculation. If you want the bottom step to sit on a foundation stone that's slightly out of the ground, also subtract this height. It's important to make these adjustments before you settle on the riser height because you can't fudge with the riser height once you begin building. People can stumble if steps rise unevenly.

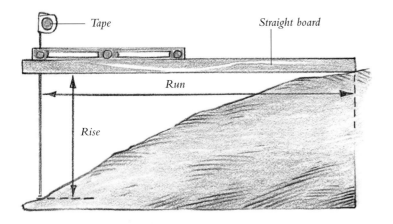

Tape

Straight board

Run

Rise

Uniform tread depth is also important, but not as critical. Divide the total run by the number of steps, then add at least a couple of inches so treads are deep enough for the back edge to support the front of the riser for the step above. If you're using relatively thin treads with separate risers, the treads should overlap the risers by 1 inch in the front.

FINE-TUNING THE DIMENSIONS If your slope is too steep to get the rise and tread depth within an acceptable range, sculpt the slope or change the stair design rather than compromise the safety of your stairs.

To make a slope less steep, make it longer. This approach works well for relatively shallow stairs. To check the new riser height and tread depth, move the stakes to their new positions, restring the twine, and redo your calculations.

Redesigning staircases on steep slopes is more complicated. To get the rise within the acceptable range, you may need to build the steps at an angle across the slope instead of going straight up. Or you can zigzag up the hill with sections of steps separated by landings. Be sure to provide adequate drainage.

To give people a place to catch their breath on long flights of stairs and to break a fall if anyone slips, divide flights of more than five steps into sections separated by a landing.

Make stairs on busy routes at least 5 feet wide. For steps that will be used infrequently, the minimum is 2 feet wide. If a path leads to steps, make them at least as wide as it is.

OTHER ISSUES There are a few more design issues to resolve before you begin building:

Plan how you'll keep dirt from washing down the slope onto your steps. Options include burying stones halfway at both sides of the steps or building a low retaining wall alongside the stairs.

With mortar, it's easy to adjust the height of steps so they're all equal. Mortar also helps seal joints between stones so that water doesn't flow in and undermine the staircase.

Also consider whether to add low-voltage lighting along the steps. If you build a retaining wall to bolster the stairs, you can incorporate lighting fixtures in it. Fixtures should cast light on treads but not shine into people's eyes. Lighting is particularly helpful when there are just a few steps along a path, because people aren't expecting them.

BUILDING SIMPLE STEPS

If you choose stone slabs that are big and thick enough, you can build a staircase just from them. Or select big slabs at least 1½ inches thick for treads and make risers from smaller stone, bricks, rot-resistant wood, concrete blocks, or other materials. Cobblestones work perfectly, since they are typically 4 or 5 inches thick. A third alternative is to use small stones for both treads and risers. Set these in mortar.

You can also build steps or a series of terraces from rot-resistant timbers and fill in around them with crushed gravel.

BUILDING STEPPING-STONE STEPS

If you need just a few steps and have a way to get large, heavy stones to the site, you can build what's called a stepping-stone staircase. Use either irregularly shaped flagstone or large blocks of cut stone. Each stone makes one step.

Select relatively flat stones at least 20 inches long, 24 inches wide, and about 6 inches thick. Buy one extra piece to serve as a foundation stone.

Starting at the bottom of the slope, dig a foundation hole as big around as the stone. Go down as deep as the stone if you live where winters are mild. If your ground freezes, excavate 4 to 6 inches deeper and pack that space with crushed gravel.

Add sand and pack it into a 2-inch layer with a hand tamper, or mist the sand to settle it thoroughly. Wait for any puddles to drain away.

Move the first stone onto the damp sand. Twist or tamp the stone until it is just slightly sloped and about 2 inches above the surrounding soil. If there is a gap behind the stone, pack it with soil or gravel.

Dig back behind the foundation stone to create enough room for the second stone, plus about an inch of sand (use more sand if the stones are bumpy). Place the next step so that it overlaps the foundation stone by at least 1 inch. To level this step, twist it into the sand or shim under the front with thin, flat stones. Fill around the shims with mortar if you wish, but don't expect mortar to glue wobbly stones together. Repeat to position other stones.

If you use thick slabs as steps, use small wedge stones and perhaps mortar to make the pieces level and stable and to adjust the stones so all steps rise an equal distance.

When all the steps are in place, dig back some of the bank alongside the steps so that you can embed large stones there to keep soil from washing down the steps.

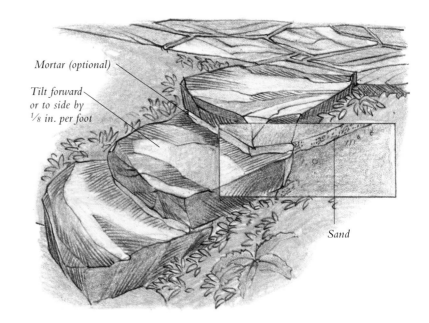

Mortar (optional)

Tilt forward or to side by ⅛ in. per foot

Sand

BUILDING STEPS OF TIMBER AND GRAVEL For stable steps, box in each tread with pressure-treated or other rot-resistant 6-by-6-inch timbers. (Wood sold as 4 by 4 is only 3½ inches thick, which is too shallow to make comfortable steps.)

Level an area for the bottom step. Build the timber frame in place. Make sure it's level. Drill holes in the front two corners and drive ½-inch galvanized pipe or ¾-inch rebar through the wood to pin it to the ground. Pound the metal a little below the top of the wood.

Excavate behind the first step to create room for the next one. Build the second frame so that its front piece rests on the back of the first frame. Drill through the overlapped corners and pound pipe or rebar through the holes. Continue in this way up the slope.

Fill the frames with crushed gravel (such as ⅝-inch with fines) and pack it in well. You can install gravel as you build each step, giving you an easier way up and down. But cover the gravel with cloths (less slippery than plastic tarps) to keep it clean while you're excavating soil for the steps above.

Gravel

6-by-6 timbers

½-in. galvanized pipe or ¾-in. rebar

Instead of framing each step in wood, you can use timbers for only the front edge of each step. But the gravel fill is more likely to wash out when steps are built this way.

BUILDING FLAGSTONE STEPS

Build these steps using 1½- to 2-inch-thick flagstones mortared together or single, large slabs. For risers, use granite cobblestones 4 or 5 inches thick or one or two layers of ledgestone. You will also need two rectangular cobblestones for support pieces on the sides of each step, plus ⅝-inch-minus crushed gravel, concrete, and mortar. The materials are small enough so that you can haul them in the family car, but it will probably take several trips. You may want to have them delivered instead.

To prepare, place the stones in tread-size arrangements. Cut them where necessary so pieces fit nicely and are separated by about ½ inch. The overall size of each tread should allow you to cover the back edge with the granite riser blocks and still leave the exposed tread depth that you want. Identify the flagstones for each tread and set them aside.

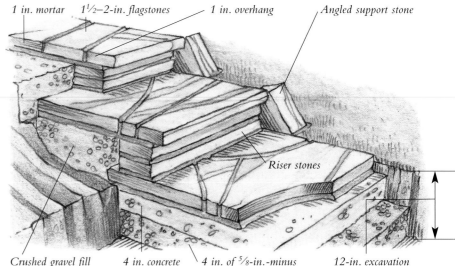

1 in. mortar   1½–2-in. flagstones   1 in. overhang   Angled support stone

Riser stones

Crushed gravel fill   4 in. concrete   4 in. of ⅝-in.-minus crushed gravel   12-in. excavation

1 Measure along the level string or board that you used to calculate the dimensions of your steps (pages 82–83) and mark the beginning and end of each tread. Transfer these marks to the ground with a mason's line (a plumb bob on a string), and drive a stake into each spot. Use a carpenter's square to lay out parallel lines and establish the other side of the steps. Drive stakes at those corners, too.

2 Excavate the rough shape of the steps.

3 Arrange flagstones for the bottom tread, which will be flush with the soil. Mark the overall outline, remove the stones, and dig down 12 inches. Pack with 4 inches of gravel.

Prepare bagged concrete mix and shovel it over the gravel, making a 4-inch layer walled in by soil. Smooth the surface (it

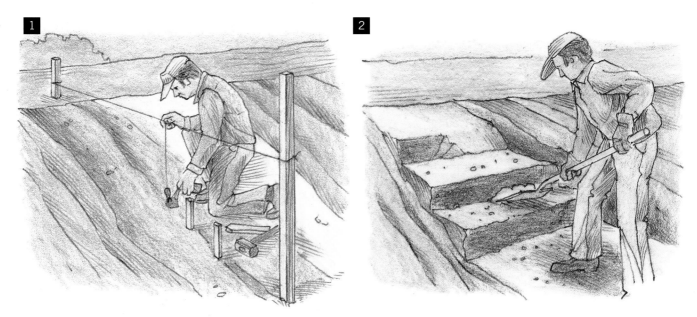

1

2

doesn't need to be perfect) and wait at least 24 hours.

4 At each side, dig out enough soil so you can place one rectangular cobblestone at a 45-degree angle to keep dirt from falling onto the steps. Set the stones far enough forward that they won't be covered up completely by the riser stones.

Prepare mortar, using either a bagged mix or a homemade batch of 1 part masonry cement to 3 parts masonry sand. Add just enough water to create a stiff mixture. Spread a 2-inch layer on the concrete and around the angled stones. Top this with the flagstones. Jiggle them slightly to set them. Tap them with a rubber mallet until they are level or tipped very slightly toward the front so that water can drain off.

With a trowel, fill spaces between stones with mortar. When it stiffens slightly, stuff it down with a trowel. Cut away

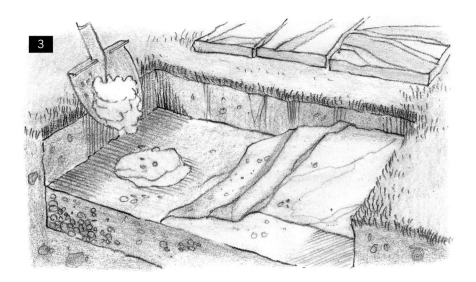

excess mortar and lift it away. Clean up residue with a damp sponge. Cover the step with plastic and wait three days.

5 To build the next step, spread a 1-inch layer of mortar as wide as the riser stones along the back of the flagstones. Place the riser stones on top and fill between them with mortar. Level the stones and wipe away smears.

After the mortar sets, carefully dig a 6-inch-deep hole behind the risers to accommodate the next step. Add 3 inches of gravel, tamp, and then add more gravel

and pack it down. Stop when the gravel is 2 inches below the top of the risers. Mix more mortar and spread a 2-inch layer over the crushed gravel. Set the flagstones for the second tread in place, with 1 inch overhanging the riser below. Tap the stones and make sure they're level.

Repeat step 5 until you reach the top of the slope.

If you see that your spacing is off as you reach the top step, don't attempt to alter the riser height. Adjust the soil level at the top of the slope to accommodate the steps.

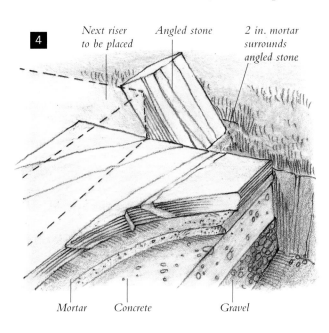

Next riser to be placed   *Angled stone*   *2 in. mortar surrounds angled stone*

Mortar   *Concrete*   *Gravel*

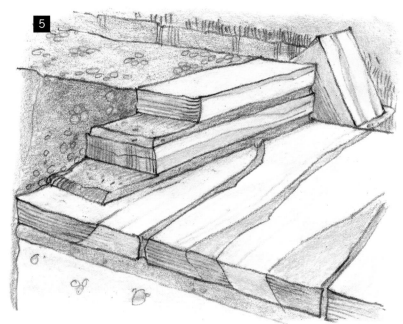

BOULDERS, ROCK GARDENS, AND WALLS

Whether your garden is large or small, you can boost its appeal by incorporating vertical rock features such as boulders, rock gardens, and stone walls. These elements provide form and substance. They also add year-round interest to gardens that otherwise might consist mostly of perennials that die back in winter.

Vertical stone features help establish a clear organizing principal for a space. This makes a garden seem more cohesive and restful. For example, if you set boulders into a weedy hillside, it almost instantly becomes the beginning of a rock garden. Stone walls carry this idea even further. By dividing a garden into areas devoted to specific purposes or gardening styles, they make each space more manageable and usable.

There is an art to using vertical rock features most effectively, as this chapter explains. If you are deciding where to place boulders or how to design a rock garden, your key concern may be to mimic ways that stone appears in natural settings. If you are building a stone wall, however, your focus will be on details that will keep the structure intact for decades.

ABOVE: *Weathered and cracked, a boulder adds a sense of permanence to a garden where a pair of olive trees will take a few more years to achieve their characteristic gnarled form. Fieldstone boulders, which have been rounded by weather or glaciers, convey a look of old age better than sharp-edged stone fresh from a quarry.*

LEFT: *A carefully composed boulder arrangement, set off by a band of small, smooth black stones, accents a parking lot. Although the boulder area consists of three parts, it appears to be part of the same bedrock formation because of the way the pieces are set.*

boulders

Boulders serve different purposes in a landscape, depending on their shape and how they are used. Low, wide stones work as anchors. Tall, skinny ones stand as sentinels. Single stones are accents, while collections of boulders suggest mountain outcroppings. With a coat of moss, a boulder helps even a newly planted landscape look as if it's been there for a long time.

You can also use stones for specific effects. In a Japanese-style garden, an upright stone may represent a mountain or an island. In a Chinese-style garden, a heavily weathered stone becomes a curiosity, drawing attention because of its contorted shape. A wide boulder with one relatively flat face can serve as an address marker if numbers or letters are painted on it. Or, if this type of boulder is set on its side, it can serve as a backrest for a bench.

Boulders are accent pieces in their own right, and they also work well to set off other garden accents. At upper right, boulders make a sitting area seem more secluded. At right, they contrast with decorative balls. Below, boulders break up a mass planting of santolina—and, in combination with fish sculptures, create the look of a seabed. The similar shapes of stone and plants add to the restful feel of this garden.

Arrangements of three, five, or seven boulders look more balanced than those with an even number of pieces. In this Zen garden, the careful positioning of stones and plants creates a serene look.

WORKING BOULDERS INTO A LANDSCAPE

In most cases, boulders look best if they're placed the way stone appears in open fields or on mountainsides. Take your cues from what you see as you drive or hike through the countryside near your home. Among the details you may discover:

- Except where glaciers dropped piles of rock or where volcanoes spit out molten stone, there is usually only one kind of stone at each site. You might want to limit your design to one type as well.
- Stones usually rise out of the ground, with just a tip or a couple of faces protruding. In your yard, you can create the same effect by burying each stone at its widest point.
- Where outcroppings of layered rock appear, they usually consist of parallel bands of stone. To arrange relatively small stones to create a similar effect, line up the stratification layers and keep the top surface of each piece on roughly the same plane. The stones should look as if they came from one piece that formed in layers on an ancient seabed and was tipped up by geologic force.
- Often, when your eye focuses on a particularly beautiful arrangement of stone in a natural setting, it's because surrounding vegetation frames the view. As you plan your landscape, evaluate whether trees or other elements offer this possibility.
- Traveling through hilly regions, a road or path follows the route of least resistance, hugging the base of hills whenever possible. Place boulders on opposite sides of a path to create this same effect.
- When you're out in the countryside, the landscape has a clear front, middle, and back, and objects in the rear appear smaller than they really are. You can make a yard seem larger by arranging several big boulders toward the front and placing a similar but smaller arrangement farther back.

Two ways of placing boulders naturally: Set outcroppings of rock in parallel bands (left) or tilt the top of each stone at the same angle (right).

Boulders look best when they rise gradually from the ground. Nature did the handiwork in the scene immediately below, where goldmoss sedum creeps across a crevice. Landscapers set boulders in the lower picture; notice how one flagstone step was cut to hug the smaller boulder.

Design Tip

To use several small stones to mimic the look of one large piece, set jagged edges up and pile soil behind the stones so they look as if they were pushed upward, out of bedrock.

SHOPPING FOR BOULDERS

If you love stone, you'll have a great time shopping for boulders at a stone yard. Take a camera and a tape measure, and allow plenty of time. Wander around and note which stones you particularly like. You may discover why people in the business often say they choose stones that "speak" to them.

Take snapshots and measurements of the stones you're considering. Back home, stuff plastic garbage bags with newspapers to create roughly the same shapes and test the effects in your yard. Remember to adjust for the part of the boulders that you'll set underground.

If you feel overwhelmed by all the choices, focus on selecting one or two large pieces that you especially love and ask the stone yard to fill in the rest of your order. In general, odd-numbered groupings of up to nine stones look best. With more stones than that, a rock collection tends to look too cluttered.

ARRANGING FOR DELIVERY

Before you buy boulders, make sure you can get them home and in place. Stone yards typically offer a variety of delivery options or can refer you to companies that do. If you request it, the delivery company may send a person out beforehand to verify that its equipment will work in your yard. A house call might also open your eyes to possibilities you hadn't considered, such as temporarily removing a side fence to create a wider opening for equipment to get into the backyard. Discuss the location of power lines, overhanging trees, and buried pipes or a septic tank when you arrange for delivery.

■ A boom truck, with a crane arm that lifts individual rocks and sets them on the ground, is usually the best option, as long as its reach fits your needs. The weight of the stones is part of the calculation: a truck that reaches 40 feet with a 1-ton stone might be able to extend

only 20 feet with a 2-ton stone. Figure on paying at least $500 for the service.
■ A crane has an even longer reach, but the cost is higher, maybe thousands of dollars.
■ A forklift or a skid-steer loader will fit through a 6-foot-wide gate. Although it's possible to rent either machine, moving boulders isn't a good first-time project. For a few hundred dollars, you can hire a skilled operator to do the job. Protect lawn from ruts by laying down sheets of plywood first.

When you shop for boulders, it's easy to fall in love with many different types of stone. But if you want a tidy garden, limit yourself to a single type and perhaps just a few carefully chosen plant varieties.

Thick slabs of red Arizona sandstone, tipped at an angle to resemble nearby mountains, cradle a plastic-lined pond.

■ You can also move boulders with the traditional, low-tech methods discussed on page 19.

Whatever method you choose, plan where the stones will be unloaded, unless the boom truck or crane will lower them directly into place. Large boulders will probably crush whatever's underneath. Avoid dumping boulders onto a septic tank or a concrete driveway. Lawn is easier to repair.

The stone yard's crew can help you position the stones, but you'll be paying for their time so excavate beforehand, if possible. Don't dig too deep; you don't want uncompacted fill underneath the stones.

Character Stones

Many stone yards sort boulders for specific uses and raise the prices accordingly. You can sometimes find similar stones in unsorted piles at lower cost. Remember that the categories are only a guide: you don't have to use a "column" stone in a vertical way, for example.

"Sign stones" have a wide horizontal face, suitable for displaying the name of a business. You might use these to display your address or as a backrest next to a stone you can sit on. You can also tip a sign stone on its side so the widest dimension runs vertically.

"Columns," or "standing stones," are long and skinny. Placed vertically, a single one makes a dramatic accent, while a group simulates a rock outcropping. Drilled, a column works well as a fountain. Tipped on a side, it becomes a garden bench or a low wall. Some stone yards carry granite columns that have been cut to shape, as well as intriguing basalt pillars that formed naturally. These pillars began as molten lava that shrank as it cooled, cracking in the most efficient geometric pattern, usually a hexagon.

"Tables" and "benches" are short columns.

"Dish stones" have a depression on one wide face, ideal for creating shallow pools, birdbaths, or butterfly watering holes.

"Moss rocks" have patches of moss or lichen, a plantlike organism made up of an alga and a fungus. Moss rocks make beautiful garden accents. But the growth, which may have taken decades to form, is fragile. Protect these rocks by placing them where they won't be used as benches or climbing structures or subjected to a steady stream of fresh water or even occasional splashes from a chlorinated swimming pool.

"Holey boulders," as the name implies, are stones, usually limestone, that are marked with holes. These are great for making a landscape look old.

Formed with a natural depression, this "dish stone" doubles as a birdbath and reflecting pool in a dreamy setting that also includes moss-covered boulders, ferns, and sweet woodruff.

"PLANTING" BIG ROCKS

Placing boulders involves more than just hauling them where you want them. You also need to "plant" each one into the ground so it looks natural.

Settle the stone so its widest circumference will be even with the top of the surrounding soil. If one side of the boulder looks weathered or shows patches of moss or lichen, that side should face up. Otherwise, place the stone with its smaller end down.

With a column, be especially careful to dig a hole that

matches the shape of the stone's base. This makes a big difference in the column's stability. About one-fourth of the column's height should be below ground. You can get by with less if the column's bottom end is cut straight off rather than left in its natural, rounded shape.

Once a boulder is in the ground, it's not easy to lift out. But you can pivot the stone or tip it slightly with a rock bar if you don't like how it looks. Place a stone or piece of wood underneath the bar to act as a fulcrum. Have a supply of rocks on hand so that you can stuff them into the hole and lock the boulder into position once you're satisfied with its placement.

PLANTING AROUND BOULDERS

Plants add to the appeal of boulders and make them look more natural. In dry areas, the best planting spots are on the shady side, where moisture is greater. Crevices between stones are also good planting spots.

Consider planting a tree that you can prune so that it eventually frames the stone. Ornamental grasses also make great companions for boulders.

Good mates for boulders include flashy Persicaria virginiana *'Painter's Palette' (at left, with a rock carving by Marcia Donahue of Berkeley, California); deer fern and bunchberry (top right); and mounding stonecrop (right).*

CREATING SPECIAL EFFECTS

Stone makes good building blocks for many creative projects. Pile pieces into interesting geometric shapes. Or recreate scenes from nature. For example, if you long for the restful effect of flowing water but don't want to add an artificial stream or pond, you can use stones to make a dry creek bed or waterfall. You might even adopt one technique from devotees of the Asian art form of *suiseki* and seek out stones streaked with white to suggest the water.

To personalize your garden, consider purchasing a carved stone or embellishing a boulder yourself. A simple design can resemble a petroglyph, with a hand, star, or other shape scratched into the surface. Or, if you have a stone whose natural shape reminds you of a face or a creature, you might add a feature or two to enhance the effect.

An ancient oak is ringed with stone to help hold deep mulch away from the bark, where persistent moisture might lead to a fungal disease. As a decorative flourish, more of the stone is piled into two pyramids.

In Japanese-style gardens, stone lanterns are prized decorative elements. They can also symbolize the presence of humans in a setting that otherwise is usually designed to look as natural as possible. Lanterns typically feature a wide brim, a holdover from the time when it was important to keep snow away from the light source, which was typically either a candle or an oil lamp.

Three ways to use stone spheres: as flanking for a sculpture (below left), as a topping for a pillar made of concrete or stone (below middle), and as a decorative insert in a stone wall (below right). Look for spheres at garden centers and stone yards.

rock gardens

Rock gardens weave stone and plants into a rich tapestry that carpets the area with color. Traditional rock gardens mimic the growing conditions typically found in alpine regions, where plants cling to pockets of soil that collect in gaps between stones. Perhaps to make up for their harsh life, these plants tend to go all out when they flower, so they are worth the extra effort to grow.

Other types of rock gardens also exist. For example, you can combine true alpines with other low-growing plants that need little water. Or you can use plants that thrive in moist shade. You can even put the emphasis on the stone rather than the plants and create a Japanese gravel garden.

RIGHT: *A sun-drenched rock garden with gravely soil provides ideal conditions for true alpines and many other flowering plants that need fast-draining soil in order to stay healthy.*

BELOW: *Japanese-style gardens often use stone in symbolic ways. Gravel stands in for water, and boulders work as miniature islands, for example.*

ABOVE: *In some rock gardens, each element is independent and distinct, as in the tidy southwestern garden (top). In other rock gardens (bottom), plants sprawl and intertwine, much as they would in a natural setting.*

RIGHT: *Lichen-crusted boulders, Japanese forest grass, and baby's tears create a rich tapestry that thrives in shade along a flagstone path.*

101

DESIGNING AND BUILDING AN ALPINE ROCK GARDEN

Alpine rock gardens are the trickiest type of garden to design because they accommodate plants that tend to rot in standard garden beds. These plants demand fast-draining soil, yet they still need an adequate amount of moisture.

To meet these conflicting demands, you need to provide four key elements: a slope, a soil mixture that drains fast yet contains a considerable amount of organic matter, a gravel mulch, and rocks spaced so you can plant in gaps where moisture will linger.

Pick a sunny location exposed to breezes. If you don't have that kind of exposure on a dry bank or a driveway that's cut into a hill, design a low, spreading mound.

To create a natural-looking rock garden, stick with a single type of stone and embed most pieces, particularly large boulders, so that they rise up from the ground. Look for opportunities to play up special features, such as natural depressions (left) or wide, flat surfaces that work as seating (above).

Remove soil to a depth of at least 18 inches. If you get a lot of summer rain, you may want to install a drainage pipe at the bottom of the hole. Extend the pipe at a downward slope to a "dry sink," a hole in the ground filled with rocks, where water can slowly seep into soil away from the rock garden.

spread 1 or 2 inches of crushed gravel over the entire rock garden, including a little around the crown of each plant. Choose any size gravel up to ¾ inch diameter, but avoid mixtures that include extremely fine particles, or "fines," because they pack down too hard.

To add plants after the gravel is in place, first clear the gravel mulch well away so it doesn't get mixed with soil.

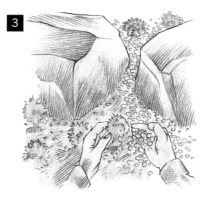

1 Work out a rough plan for placing your boulders. If you want them to look like part of one natural outcropping, make the grain or layers run in one direction, and make the tops tilt at a uniform angle. Use stones of different sizes, and vary the spacing between them.

2 Install any boulders that you want to rest on the bottom of the excavation or that need to be embedded even deeper. Then spread a 6-inch-thick layer of drainage material over the remaining bottom of the excavation. Use rocks, broken bricks,

or chunks of old concrete. Over that, position the remaining large stones. Fill in around them and build up the mound with gritty soil. A typical mix has equal parts loamy topsoil, crushed gravel, and organic material such as leaf mold or compost. You may need to add acidic or alkaline soil amendments to meet the needs of specific plants.

3 Arrange the plants while they are still in their pots. When you like the effect, begin planting. Set the top of each root ball about ½ inch above the eventual height of your rock garden. Then

PLANTING A ROCK GARDEN

Because rock gardens are miniature representations of mountain terrain, compact plants that make tidy mounds generally look best. Plant the most drought-tolerant species near the top of your slope or mound and the ones that need more water lower down. If you choose true alpine plants, remember that they are used to living a tough life. Water infrequently but deeply, preferably with soaker hoses or a drip system so the foliage doesn't get wet. Do not overfertilize.

Besides the plants listed here, you may also want to consider plants suitable for planting between stepping-stones (pages 20–21), in gravel (pages 30–31), and along flagstone paths (pages 50–51).

Rugged red rocks bring out the vivid colors in a collection of succulents. By elevating the planting area, the rocks also help ensure the fast-draining soil that these plants demand.

Alpine columbine

Aquilegia alpina / Hardy everywhere. Full sun to light shade. Regular water. Bright blue 2-inch flowers with curved, nectar-producing spurs flutter on stems 1–2 feet tall over lacy foliage. Flowers attract hummingbirds. Cut off spent blooms to get a second flush of flowers.

Alpine columbine

Coral bells

Heuchera / Hardy everywhere. Light shade. Regular water. Coral bells do well in sunny rock gardens. Heucherella hybrids combine the flowering habit of coral bells with the heart-shaped leaves of foamflower *(Tiarella cordifolia).*

Dwarf Alberta spruce

Picea glauca albertiana 'Conica' / Hardy to –30°F/–34°C. Full sun or light shade. Little to moderate water. Compact, cone-shaped shrub reaches 6–8 feet tall and 4–5 feet wide in 35 years, so it's for spacious rock gardens only. Needs shelter from drying winds and strong reflected sunlight.

Dwarf daffodil

Narcissus / Hardy to –30°F/–34°C. Full sun during spring bloom, light shade afterward. Regular water during growth and bloom. Look for dwarf forms about 6 inches tall, including 'Tête-à-tête' and 'Jumblie', both with yellow flowers.

Garland daphne

Daphne cneorum / Hardy to –20°F/ –29°C. Full sun, but part shade where summers are hot. Moderate water. Clusters of fragrant, rosy pink flowers appear in spring on branches that form mounds 1 foot tall by 3 feet wide. All parts are poisonous. Top-dress with peat moss and sand after bloom.

Sunrose

Lewisia

Hardy everywhere. Full sun or light shade. Little to moderate water. These Western natives have extremely showy flowers. Bitterroot *(L. rediviva),* Montana's state flower, has 2-inch flowers that look like water lilies. *L. cotyledon,* from Northern California and Oregon, has 1-inch flowers from spring to early summer. All types require excellent drainage.

Rockcress

Arabis × sturii / Hardy everywhere. Full sun. Moderate water. This low-growing, spreading evergreen is considered by some to be the finest rock garden plant. Dense, fist-size cushions of bright green leaves form small mats. Clusters of white flowers appear on 2–3 inch stems in spring.

Saxifrage

Saxifraga / Hardiness and sun exposure vary. Regular water. From low, compact foliage, stems shoot up to carry white, pink, or red blossoms. Although most types grow in full sun to light shade, some—including strawberry geranium *(S. stolonifera)* and *S. umbrosa*—thrive in full shade.

Stonecrop

Sedum / Hardiness varies. Full sun or partial shade. Little to moderate water. These succulents vary greatly in form. For rock gardens, select small types, such as *S. brevifolium,* which has ⅛-inch leaves packed onto stems just 2–3 inches tall, or *S. spathulifolium,* with ½- to 1-inch spoon-shaped leaves that form rosettes on short, trailing stems.

Trailing phlox

Sunrose

Helianthemum nummularium / Hardy to −20°F/−29°C. Full sun. Moderate water. These plants produce sure-fire color, with flowers in bright or pastel colors, ranging from red or orange to pink or white. From midspring through early summer, they play off the gray or glossy green leaves. Plants grow 6–8 inches tall and spread 3 feet wide.

Trailing phlox

Phlox nivalis / Hardy to −22°F/−30°C. Full sun or light shade. Regular water. This plant is native to the central United States. It forms a loose mat 4–6 inches tall and 1 foot wide. Large clusters of pink or white flowers appear in late spring or early summer. Requires excellent drainage.

A backyard garden based on Japanese design ideas packs several pathways, a lawn, and wilder areas into a small space.

CREATING A JAPANESE-STYLE ROCK GARDEN

With their exquisite balance of space and mass, Japanese-style rock gardens invite contemplation and create a serene atmosphere. In these gardens, gravel often stands in for water. To make "waves" or "ripples," the gardener rakes the gravel into precise patterns, often looping around large, upright boulders that suggest islands or mountains.

THE PERFECT GRAVEL To hold crisp edges, the gravel in a Japanese-style rock garden must be sharp edged, not round. But it should not include the tiny pieces known as fines or it might pack down too firmly. The color is also an issue. Pure white gravel can be hard on the eyes. Crushed granite, a salt-and-pepper mix of white and black, looks more attractive. It needs to be screened so that most particles fall within a relatively narrow size range; the size to aim for can be as small as ⅛ inch or as large as ½ inch, depending on the look you want. You can also combine several sizes, as long as the smallest pieces don't fall below ⅛ inch.

Shop for gravel at companies that specialize in sand and gravel, or ask for poultry grit at a feed store. The type sold for chickens is about ⅛ inch diameter; turkey grit is about ⅜ inch.

SELECTING PLANTS FOR A JAPANESE-STYLE GARDEN

Some traditional Japanese dry gardens are devoid of plants, creating a sharp contrast between the human-made gravel landscape and a natural setting. But other Japanese-style gardens incorporate a wide range of plants, often grown more for their form than for their flower color.

- Compact evergreens work particularly well, especially if they have the gnarled, open branches common to bonsai trees. Mugho pine *(Pinus mugo mugo)* stays under 4 feet and is hardy to −60°F/−51°C. *Cedrus deodara* 'White Imp', a dwarf form of deodar cedar, reaches only 3 feet tall and has silvery green needles with cream-colored tips. It's hardy to −15°F/−26°C.

- As an accent, consider a single deciduous tree or bush with a strong horizontal branch structure, such as a Japanese maple *(Acer palmatum),* a pagoda dogwood *(Cornus alternifolia),* or a star magnolia *(Magnolia stellata).* All are hardy to −34°F/−31°C.

- Mass a single species around the base of a tree or bush. Select low-growing plants that look tidy, such as *Sedum,* which includes types hardy to −60°F/ −51°C, or Pacific iris *(Iris douglasiana),* which survives down to −15°F/−26°C. Also consider prostrate forms of juniper, such as *Juniperus chinensis* 'Parsonii' and *J. horizontalis* 'Plumosa'. Juniper is hardy everywhere.

The Rake

To create ripples in the gravel, you need to rake it with widely spaced tines. Use a garden fork or a gravel rake. Or make your own wooden rake from a broom handle, a scrap of 2 by 4, and a few short pieces of 1-inch dowel. Drill holes into the 2 by 4 to hold the dowels and the handle, making the holes slightly undersized. Slot one end of each dowel and the handle lengthwise so the wood compresses when you jam the pieces into the holes. Dribble a little wood glue around the holes' edges first.

LEFT: *Raked into precise squares, the gravel topping on this* karesansui *(dry landscape) garden reflects light differently as the sun's position changes.*

BELOW: *Like currents in a stream, ripples in sand create a sense of energy that contrasts with the stillness of the stones.*

walls

Stone walls create a powerful sense of shelter in a garden. By defining boundaries, they make large or open spaces seem more intimate. Stone walls also add comfort when they screen out noise and wind, or hold a hillside back from a patio or other garden area. Because stone is solid, stone walls also make a garden seem more substantial. And as backdrops for planting areas, they create a sharp contrast in textures that somehow always seems to make the plants look more lush.

LEFT: *Artistic embellishments add to the charm of rock walls. A carved piece was incorporated into a wall (top left). An ironwork grill fills an opening (top right). And a wall with niches provides places for ornaments, such as an oversize acorn (bottom).*

There are infinite ways to stack stones into walls. For the steep hillside garden pictured above, the owners needed a massive retaining wall. But by breaking it into short sections interspersed with planting beds, they wound up with a structure that looks more like a terraced garden. At left, a single row of large stones surrounds a planting bed and creates informal seating areas.

DESIGNING STONE WALLS

Stone walls can be tall or low; they can curve or run in crisp, straight lines. Whatever their style, they make a significant statement in a landscape. Try out possible designs by positioning hoses, extension cords, or stakes and string in a double row, which will simulate the substantial width of stone walls. If you have trouble visualizing how the walls would change the feel of your garden, set out cardboard boxes. Stack them to experiment with different heights.

The quintessential stone wall is dry-stacked—meaning only gravity and friction hold its pieces in place. Other options include a mortared stone wall or a veneered wall, the latter of which consists

If you're building with round river rock, use mortar between joints rather than attempt a dry-stacked wall.

of thin slabs of natural stone mortared over concrete blocks or other core material.

Dry-stacked walls need to be at least 2 feet wide at the base to be stable, but they don't need much of a foundation. If you plan to build the wall yourself or with helpers who are relatively inexperienced, this is the best option.

Mortared and veneered walls can be narrower than dry-stacked ones, thus saving space. But they need substantial foundations and usually require more expert labor. If you want a tall wall or a heavy-duty retaining wall and live where earthquake safety is an issue, a veneered wall is a particularly good choice because reinforcing can be added to the core structure.

Pillars of smooth cut stone contrast with the rougher texture of the main material in this wall. Note the capstones, which are tightly butted together vertically instead of being placed horizontally. With either style, each capstone should span the full thickness of the wall.

SHOPPING FOR STONE

With dry-stacked or mortared walls, you can use the same type of stone for all three parts: the foundation, the main expanse of wall, and the cap. But you may want to select different materials for each part:

- Because the foundation will be hidden, you may save money or time by building it from concrete blocks, poured concrete, or less expensive stone than you will use for the rest of the wall.
- For the main expanse of a dry-stacked wall, you can use larger stones along the inside and outside faces and fill the middle mostly with smaller stones. If you have a lot of small rocks on your property, this is a good way to use them. You can do the same thing with a mortared wall, although you can also use smaller stones throughout.
- For the cap, choose large, heavy pieces if you have a dry-stacked wall. Capstones that span several underlying stones will make the wall far more stable. With a mortared wall, capstone size isn't as critical, but large pieces still look best. Use bluestone pavers or other cut stone if you want a tailored appearance. For a more casual look, consider tumbled pavers.

At a stone yard, you may find roughly shaped cubes, bricks, and slabs of the same type of stone labeled in various ways. This is what the terms signify:

FLAGSTONE, SLATE, BLUESTONE Fairly flat pieces generally 1 to 2 inches thick. Primarily used for paving, these also make good wall material and excellent capstones. For wall stone, naturally broken edges look best, although for capstones, sawn edges are also fine.

TUMBLED Any of the above after sharp edges are knocked off by tumbling the stone in a mixer. Tumbled stone looks worn and aged; it works well for both wall material and capstones.

ASHLAR Square or rectangular blocks, often with flat tops, bottoms, and ends, but with textured sides (the only faces visible in a wall). Split ashlar exposes the natural layers of the stone on the sides. Sawn bed ashlar is almost perfectly flat on the top and bottom because these surfaces are cut with a saw; it's a good choice if you want a neat-looking wall.

FIELDSTONE Literally "stone found in a field." For dry-stacked walls, look for relatively flat pieces, similar to what you might use for stepping-stones. Thin, circular

Neatly stacked fieldstone makes a fine planting bed for a maple tree. For the corner, the builder picked out pieces with two flat sides or shaped the stones to create that tidy look.

fieldstone, often sold as "flats," makes good veneer.

RUBBLE Broken pieces of stone. Although the term implies that the pieces are random sizes, you may find pallets loaded with rubble that is relatively flat and square, ideal for a stone wall.

Bring dimensions of your project with you when you shop. Ask the stone yard's staff to help you calculate how much to order. Be sure to include materials for the foundation, and order a little extra. Some stone yards post the square feet that a ton of material will cover. Be aware that this refers to the area on only one side of the wall, such as for a retaining wall. Freestanding walls have two sides, so you'll need twice as much.

BUILDING A DRY-STACKED WALL

The best dry-stacked walls are built with big, heavy pieces of stone. Minimize lifting by having materials delivered close to where you will need them. If you are using one type of stone throughout, sort pieces before you build. Save the flattest pieces for the top and those with square edges for corners or ends. Use ugly pieces with one relatively flat face for the foundation. Keep small, wedge-shaped stones to chink gaps or steady wobbly stones.

These directions apply to a wall less than 4 feet tall:

1 Mark the perimeter of the wall's base with stakes and string. Dig down several inches to remove sod and roots.

Place foundation stones with their flattest side up. Excavate as necessary so the tops lie even with adjoining soil and slightly slant toward the wall's center. If you dig too deep, refill with finely crushed gravel or masonry sand; soil won't compact properly. Leave a few inches between the stones, and fill the gaps with gravel to help water drain.

2 Lay the first course, working from the outsides in. Place stones with the nicest sides out and their tops slightly slanted toward the center of the wall. Fill any gaps at the center with smaller or less attractive stones.

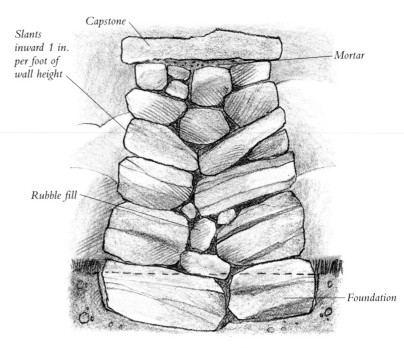

Slants inward 1 in. per foot of wall height

Capstone

Mortar

Rubble fill

Foundation

3 As you build, check each piece to make sure it sits securely and fits well with neighboring stones. Chip off bumps or reshape edges using the techniques on pages 45 and 57. If stones wobble, stuff small pieces into gaps. Tap the chinking into place from the inside or the outside of the wall.

4 Set the next courses in the same way, staggering the joints so they don't line up vertically. Adhere to the stonemason's rule "Two stones over one, and one stone over two."

5 Every 6 to 8 feet along the wall, set a tie piece—a stone placed with its long dimension

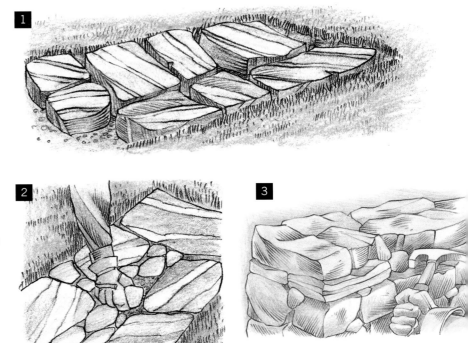

When stones vary in thickness, stack several thin pieces to match the height of an adjoining thick slab so that the overall look results in horizontal lines across the wall.

6 After the final course, add capstones. If they are big enough to span the wall's thickness, just place them on top and add whatever shim stones are necessary. If you must use smaller capstones, pack mortar into the joints so water doesn't run down into the wall. With either large or small capstones, boost the wall's strength by spreading mortar on the top course of wall stones. Lower the capstones into that. Use a bagged mortar mix or a homemade batch of 1 part masonry cement to 3 parts sand, plus just enough water to make a stiff mix. Wait for the mortar to stiffen slightly before you smooth it and lift off any excess. Clean away any mortar spills with a damp sponge.

perpendicular to the direction of the wall—to interconnect the front and back of the wall. Set the first tie piece so it projects inward from one side of wall, the next one so it projects inward from the opposite side, and so on for the length of the wall. If possible, use pieces that span the wall's width. Otherwise, select pairs of stones that each reach three-quarters of the way across. Set them so they project inward from opposite sides of the wall and butt them together tightly. Also interlock stones at corners and wall ends by setting stones in each new layer so their long dimension is at a 90-degree angle to pieces of the layer before. Continue to stagger the joints.

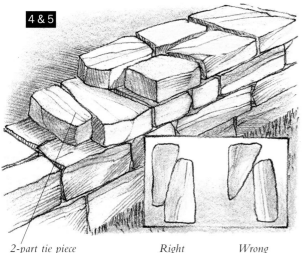

4 & 5

2-part tie piece   *Right*   *Wrong*

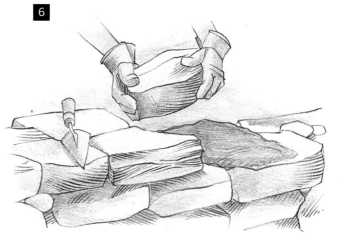

6

DESIGNING A MORTARED WALL

Mortar in a stone wall is a little like accessory jewelry: it can look cheap or elegant or be barely noticeable, depending on the style you chose.

The cheap version features wide, uneven joints where mortar is smeared over the face of the stones. Hallmarks of the elegant option are narrow, even joints neatly recessed behind the stones, details possible only when a mason fits stones as carefully as for a dry-stacked wall.

In the minimalist approach, mortar is kept back from the outside edges of the face stones so that it's barely visible. You might choose this option if you want the look of a dry-stacked wall but don't have the space for one. A straight mortared wall less than 3 feet tall, or a curved mortared wall less than 4 feet tall, can be as

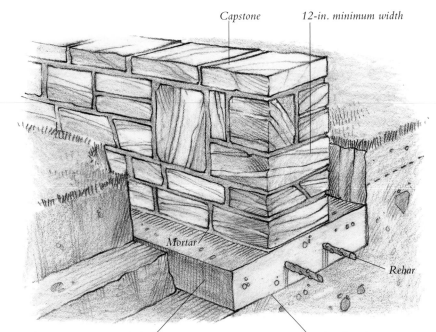

Capstone   *12-in. minimum width*

Mortar

Rebar

Concrete: at least 6 in. thick; width of wall plus 6 in., or to local code

Below frost line

little as 12 inches wide—half the thickness of a dry-stacked wall 3 feet tall.

BUILDING A MORTARED WALL

Building a mortared wall involves most of the same steps as building a dry-stacked wall (pages 112–113), with a few adaptations:

1 For the footing, dig below the frost line if you live where the ground freezes or at least a foot deep in mild areas. Make the hole 6 inches wider than the wall base, or whatever the local

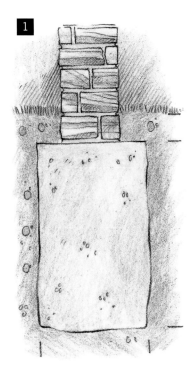

Combination Approach

A method known as "dry-appearing" construction gives you most of the stability of a mortared wall while still keeping the easy-to-build foundation of a dry-stacked wall. Build the bottom portion of the wall as you would any dry-stacked wall. When you get to the top foot or so, add mortar between stones, but keep it well back

from the face so that it doesn't show. Bed the capstones in mortar and add mortar between pieces.

Because the bottom portion of the wall will shift a bit as the ground freezes and thaws, some cracks will appear in the mortar. Inspect the wall each year and patch the mortar as necessary.

With deeply recessed mortar joints, this freestanding stone wall remains stable even without large capstones.

building code dictates. Fill the bottom of the hole with at least 6 inches of freshly prepared concrete.

If the footing needs to be quite deep, the easiest method is to dig a trench (with a backhoe or trenching machine if possible) and then fill all but the top 6 inches with concrete. Allow it to harden for a few days before you begin building.

Trial-fit stones for about 4 feet of the first course. Align them as you would in a dry-stacked wall but leave a uniform gap between pieces, especially on the outside faces. Remove the stones but keep them in the same order. Dampen them.

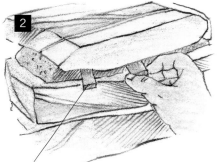

Temporary leveling wedge

Remove wedges; fill gaps with mortar

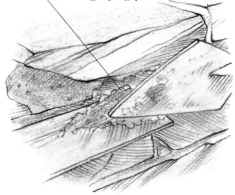

2 Mix the mortar. Use a bagged mix or a homemade batch of 1 part masonry cement to 3 parts sand, plus just enough water to make a stiff mixture. Spread a 1-inch layer of mortar over the section of the foundation and set the stones in place. Pack joints with mortar as you go. Also pack mortar around small stones in the wall's interior. Wipe away spilled mortar promptly with a damp sponge.

3 Complete the first course, or stop after a few more sections and then add additional layers. Stagger joints and install tie pieces every 6 to 8 feet, just as you would with a dry-stacked wall (see step 5 on pages 112–113).

When the mortar no longer smears, which may take half an hour or several hours, depending on the weather, shape the mortar with a bricklayer's pointing tool or a wire brush. If you wish, remove just enough mortar so that it is recessed slightly behind the face of the stones. Cover the wall with plastic for several days so that the mortar dries slowly. In dry weather, lift the plastic and mist the wall periodically.

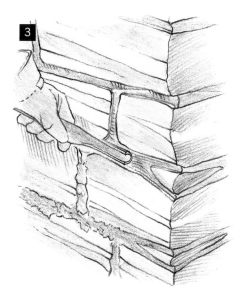

DESIGNING A VENEERED WALL

There are two types of natural stone veneer, and you can use either of them to face a retaining wall or a freestanding wall built of concrete block. Artificial stone, made with Portland cement and pumice, is also an option.

Standard veneer, which has been available for years, is real rock that's usually 4 to 6 inches thick but sometimes as much as 8 inches. It weighs less than the full-size stones it mimics, but it's still heavy enough to need a foundation, and it must be anchored to concrete blocks with noncorrosive metal wall ties. Shaping pieces so they fit tightly is similar to shaping larger stone, so the work goes relatively slowly.

Thin natural veneer, which is now available in both flat and corner pieces, is also real stone, but it's typically only ¾ to 1¾ inches thick. It costs more

Veneer stone   Mortar   Capstone   Concrete block

Anchor with wire tie   Vertical steel at center of wall

per square foot than standard veneer does, but it's so much easier to work with that the installed price often winds up lower. It's also easier for you to shape and install, if you do the work yourself. You can cut pieces with a tile or brick saw, and you don't need a foundation or ties.

Artificial stone veneer weighs (and costs) less and is as easy to install as thin natural veneer, but a trained eye can tell it's not as bright or textured as real stone.

BUILDING WITH STANDARD VENEER

Covering a concrete block wall with standard veneer is similar to building a thin stone wall from scratch, except that you need to tie it into the block wall. If you are building the block wall from scratch, you can insert metal pieces known as wall ties into mortar joints while the mortar is still pliable. Or if the wall already exists, attach the wall ties with masonry screws or powder-actuated fasteners. Stagger fasteners every 16 inches vertically and horizontally, or whatever local codes dictate. Thread 15-inch wire ties, bent as shown, through the anchors.

Because a veneer wall is just like a thin stone wall, it needs a

Thick veneer

Thin veneer

With a veneered wall, work out placement of the stones and make any necessary cuts before you prepare the mortar so it doesn't become too stiff before you can use it.

foundation. If the foundation for the block wall is wide enough, you can rest the first course of veneer stones directly on that. Otherwise, attach galvanized steel angle iron to the bottom of the block wall and rest the veneer on metal.

Build the wall as you would a freestanding mortared stone wall. As you place each stone, stuff mortar behind it to stick the veneer to the blocks. As you reach an area with a wall tie, bend the wires around the stone and mortar over them. If the stones are so heavy that they push out the mortar underneath, insert temporary wooden wedges to hold the stones apart. Once the mortar stiffens, remove the wedges and plug the holes with mortar.

BUILDING WITH THIN VENEER

Covering a concrete block wall with thin veneer—natural or man-made—is similar, except that you don't need to worry about the foundation or ties.

Arrange veneer stones on the ground to work out a design you like. If the wall includes exposed corners, place corner pieces first so you don't have to cut them. Corner pieces have a long and a short side; alternate the sides as you go up the wall.

On the infill pieces, make any necessary cuts using a tile or brick saw with water, or a diamond or abrasive blade in a circular saw or an angle grinder. Wear eye and ear protection, as well as a mask if you will generate dust.

If you use artificial stone, you may be able to trim pieces with a hatchet and wide-mouth nippers. Dampen natural stone and let it drain before cutting. (Artificial stone is often less porous, so you can mist the back of each piece as you work.)

Prepare mortar as you would for a freestanding stone wall. Many types of veneer can be installed from the top down, which reduces mortar smears.

To test, butter the back of a sample with mortar and press the piece onto a concrete block. If the sample slips, start at the bottom. Layered stone should also be installed from the bottom up or it won't look right.

Install corner pieces first, then work toward the center of the wall. As you press the mortared pieces to the blocks, mortar should ooze out around the stone and fill the joints. Repeat with additional stones. As you complete a section, check joints and add mortar where necessary, applying it with a grout bag. Wipe accidental smears off natural stone with a damp sponge. But if you are using man-made stone, wait for the mortar to become crumbly and then whisk it off with a dry bristle brush.

When the mortar stiffens a bit, use a brick jointer or a pointed trowel to compact mortar in the joints and to lift out excess material. Recessing the mortar ½ to ¾ inch adds a nice textural effect.

Add capstones that overlap the top of the wall by 1 inch and mortar them in place. Check the tops with a level. Keep the wall damp for at least several days.

DESIGNING A RETAINING WALL

Retaining walls range from hefty structures designed to hold back hillsides to low edging around elevated planting areas. Do-it-yourselfers can build simple dry-stacked stone walls less than 3 feet tall on a gentle slope with good soil, but consult your local building department to determine whether you need a building permit and soil analysis.

For a heavy-duty retaining wall, get professional design assistance and consider hiring professionals to build the structural wall with concrete blocks and rebar. If you wish, you can then face the wall with veneer stone on your own.

Of course, if your yard is flat, you're free to build a low stone planter and fill it with soil to create a welcome elevation shift.

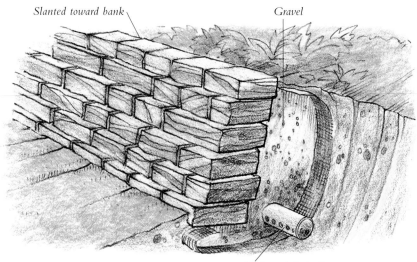

Slanted toward bank *Gravel*

Perforated drainpipe

BUILDING A SIMPLE DRY-STACKED RETAINING WALL

Think of a retaining wall as a one-sided, dry-stacked wall. Begin with a foundation course of stones set below the surface of the soil, as shown on page 112. Slant the top surface of the stones toward the bank. Dig out enough soil behind the wall so that you can install a drainage system.

Pack a little gravel at the bottom, then install drainpipe (hole side down). Slant the pipe to drain in the direction you want. Pack gravel into the rest of the space as you add layers. Set each new layer farther back toward the hillside. A 3-foot-tall wall should step back at least 6 inches total. Top with capstones, as you would a freestanding dry-stacked wall.

When you build a retaining wall, look for opportunities to incorporate other features, such as steps or planting beds.

Modular Retaining Walls

To achieve the rustic look of a dry-stacked retaining wall without having to fit the pieces together like a jigsaw puzzle, you may want to consider a modular retaining wall built from interlocking concrete blocks. The pieces come in set sizes and they interlock in such a way that the wall automatically steps back the correct amount from one course to the next.

Choose a style with a rough front face if you want the wall to resemble stone. If you want greenery to eventually cover the wall, choose blocks with a hollow center for soil and plants.

Installation is straightforward. If you want a straight wall, string mason's twine to mark the front edge. Dig a trench big enough so that you can install a 6-inch gravel layer under the first course and have 6 to 8 inches of gravel behind the blocks, or whatever the manufacturer recommends. Compact the base with a hand tamper or, even better, a motorized plate compactor. Check that the base is level.

Lay the foundation row of blocks. If the blocks have a rear lip, install the first row upside down and backward, as shown. Where drainage is an issue, lay perforated drainpipe, hole side down, on the gravel. Slope the pipe downhill to the area where you want the water to drain out.

Lay the second row of blocks, staggering the joints in a running bond pattern. Backfill the space behind the wall with gravel, and tamp the gravel firmly. Place subsequent rows of blocks in the same manner, backfilling and compacting the gravel after laying each row.

For systems that don't include capstones, manufacturers often recommend spreading a bead of construction adhesive on the top of the second-to-last row and then lowering the top row onto that.

If you're using drainpipe, lay landscape fabric over the gravel backfill before you replace the topsoil and plant behind the wall. The fabric will help prevent soil from clogging the gravel backfill and drainpipe.

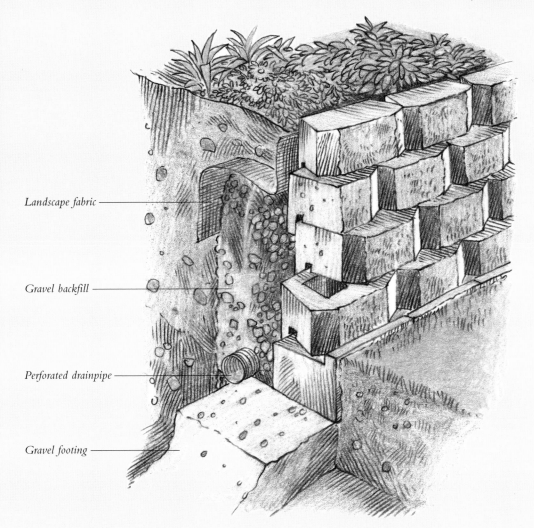

Landscape fabric

Gravel backfill

Perforated drainpipe

Gravel footing

WATER FEATURES

Water, transparent and reflective, is a natural complement to solid, still stone. Together, they create some of the most beautiful scenes in nature.

It's not surprising that many people seek to recreate this magical partnership at home. Whether simple or elaborate, well-built water features are remarkably effective in transforming a garden and bringing it to life.

Even a simple stone bowl filled with water offers a sapphire blue reflection of the sky and invites dragonflies to hover nearby or butterflies to stop for a sip. More elaborate water features often engage several senses at once. A small stone fountain, for example, encourages you to delight in the sparkle of water droplets even as you listen to the soothing sound of trickling water.

This chapter explores the many ways stone and water can be combined in a garden and discusses some of the practical and safety issues involved. You will also find detailed building plans for a wide array of water features, ranging from a child-friendly pebble fountain to a pond with a gushing waterfall.

choosing a water feature

People and wildlife are drawn toward water, which comes alive with ripples at the slightest breeze. If you decide to add a fountain, pond, or other water feature in your garden, locate it where you can see it from indoors, if possible. That way, you can enjoy its serenity and the creatures it draws even when the weather is cold. If you entertain outdoors in good weather, make the water feature easily accessible from your patio or deck as well. Your guests will have something to explore and chat about as they nibble on your treats.

If your space or budget is tight, consider a simple water feature such as a fountain or a water bowl. Elaborate streams and waterfalls constructed with large boulders are dramatic additions— and often cost thousands of dollars.

A large water feature can overpower a small yard. But in a large yard, a petite water bowl can go almost unnoticed (except by birds and other wildlife). For the best visual effect, keep your water feature in good proportion to the size of your yard, and try to integrate it with other stone work so it doesn't look tacked on.

SAFETY

If very young children may visit your yard, consider their safety as you decide how to incorporate water in your garden. Some features, such as water bowls, pose minimal risk, even for toddlers. Ponds, streams, and waterfalls are a different story. To be satisfying, they should allow easy access right to the water's edge. But toddlers don't understand the danger.

Many safety experts recommend fencing and a locking gate around ponds and similar water features. Covering the water with netting is another solution. If you're unwilling to take these steps, at least provide a gradual slope in the accessible parts of your pond or stream so that a child who falls in can climb out. When a toddler does visit, tell responsible adults what's in your yard and make sure that they supervise the child closely.

Elevated ponds, whether large (below left) or small (below, with a concrete leaf fountain) allow you to view fish or plants close-up.

Water features can be quite elaborate, with koi and sophisticated filters to keep the water crystal-clear (left). But simple designs, such as the boulder-top basin below, also can be quite satisfying and are often a better choice where young children play. See page 127 for tips on how to create a similar setup.

RIGHT: *In areas where raccoons are a problem, ponds need steep sides or the fish are likely to disappear. Adding hiding places for the fish also helps protect them. A large submerged rock propped against another one serves that purpose here.*

The interplay of light and water adds greatly to the beauty of a fountain. The builder of the fountain above incorporated lighting into the design to focus attention on the moving water even at twilight. The fountains at left are lit by natural sunlight, which makes each droplet appear to sparkle.

fountains

Fountains add greatly to the pleasures of a garden because they engage several of our senses at once. A fountain's spray sparkles in sunlight, and it cools the nearby air. The sound of water gurgling, splashing, or dripping mesmerizes people and attracts birds. Fountains also mask irritating sounds, such as traffic noise from a nearby road.

Luckily, many fountains are so simple that you can get one up and running in a day. Because it's likely to become a focal point in your garden, choose a style that will serve as an attractive garden ornament even when the water is turned off.

Home and garden centers carry many ready-made fountains. Ones that match the style of your house and garden will look best. You can also purchase the parts separately and use them to build a fountain that features natural stone. If you use the same type of stone elsewhere in your garden, your fountain will look at home from the minute you turn it on.

Stones are often used to anchor fountain vessels to the landscape. The vessels shown here include an oversize urn (above), a cast stone fountain (below left), and a drain tile topped by a planter (below right). All three are plumbed much like the pebble and boulder fountains shown on pages 126 and 127.

DESIGNING A STONE FOUNTAIN

No matter what its design, a stone fountain has just a few working parts: a bowl, a pump, and tubing that leads to a fountain device, such as a spray nozzle or a spout.

Although you can rig up a solar-powered pump, most fountains run on electricity. This requires a ground-fault-protected (GFCI) outlet with a waterproof cover close enough so you don't need an extension cord. Avoid stringing the cord where someone might trip on it or accidentally cut it with a spade. Hide the cord and tubing behind stones or plants. Both designs shown here are wonderful solutions if you have small children and want them to experience the delights of splashing water without the risk of falling into it.

BUILDING A PEBBLE FOUNTAIN

A pebble fountain consists of an underground basin topped by a grate that's covered with decorative stones. A pump in the basin sprays water up over the stones; the water drains through the stones back into the basin. The effect is particularly dazzling when sunlight hits the water droplets and makes them sparkle.

For a grate, thick wire mesh works well. The grate should be large enough to overlap the basin by at least 6 inches all around. When you buy the pump,

also shop for a fountain nozzle, a piece of rigid pipe, and whatever adapters you need to connect one end of the pipe to the pump's outlet and the other end to the nozzle.

To build the fountain, dig a hole and fill it with a plastic liner, a preformed pond shell, or any other watertight container that's open at the top and at least 15 inches deep and 18 inches wide. Add water. As the basin fills, pack sand into any crevices around the outside.

Place the pump on the bottom of the basin near the center. Point the pump's outlet hole up. Temporarily set the grate and a typical-size stone over part of the basin and measure the distance between the outlet and the top of the stone. Cut rigid pipe to match this dimension.

Remove the pump from the water and attach the pipe. To the other end of the pipe, attach the nozzle. Set the pump back into the water and position the grate over the basin. Cut a small hole in it for the fountain. Near one edge, cut a second opening big enough to reach through in case you need to adjust the pump. Top this hole with another piece of mesh that overlaps the grate enough so that it doesn't sag.

Place a few stones on the mesh and check the fountain's height. If the nozzle is below the top of the stones, set the pump on a clean brick. If the nozzle is too high, trim the pipe.

Turn on the pump and adjust the nozzle and pump pressure until all of the spray lands over the basin. When you like the effect, add the rest of the stones. (If young children will be using your garden, include pieces too heavy for them to move.) Refill the basin frequently so that the water level never drops below the top of the pump.

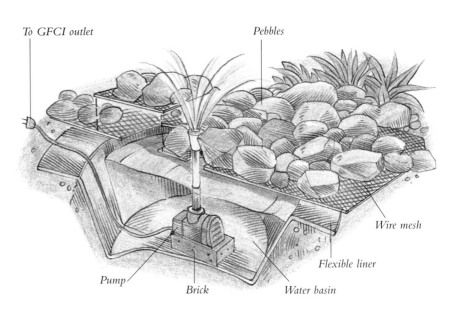

To GFCI outlet   Pebbles   Wire mesh   Flexible liner   Pump   Brick   Water basin

BUILDING A BOULDER FOUNTAIN

Some stone suppliers sell boulders already drilled for a fountain pipe or will drill a boulder that you select. Or you can rent a hammer drill and use a masonry bit to do the job yourself—although drilling stone this way takes a lot of time. Wear ear protectors and goggles.

Assembly is similar to making a pebble fountain, except that you need to pile concrete blocks in the basin as supports under the boulder. Protect the bottom of the basin by adding liner protection fabric or scraps of liner. If you want the fountain to gurgle and bubble rather than spray, you don't need a fitting on the pipe that carries water up through the stone. If you want droplets, add a nozzle.

A boulder fountain can consist of a single stone (left) or several (right). By placing stones on top of the gushing water, you can adjust the sound of the fountain.

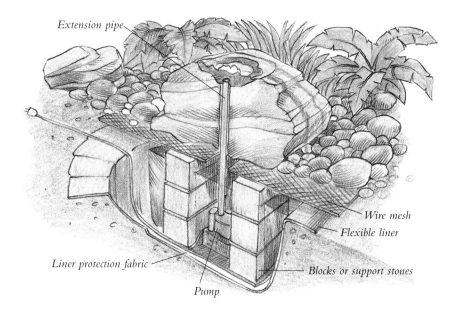

Extension pipe

Wire mesh

Flexible liner

Liner protection fabric

Blocks or support stones

Pump

ponds and pools

Whether your pond or pool is designed as a home for fish, a surface to reflect light, or a place for your family to swim, you can increase its appeal by incorporating stone into your design. Stone edging is one obvious place to start. Another possibility is placing a wide, flat boulder by the edge to serve as a jumping-off platform for a swimming pool or an observation post for a pond. If afternoon sun reaches the stone in spring or fall, you'll have a warm spot to watch the pond at twilight. You can also place a boulder in the middle of a pond, as a sort of miniature island.

As you design your pool or pond, think about whether you want to build it above ground with raised edging that doubles as a bench (top left), or dug into the ground, perhaps with the edging expanded to create a patio wide enough for lounging chairs (bottom left).

Ponds and Wildlife

Raccoons, herons, river otters, and many other creatures are likely to visit your pond to drink and dine. You may want to add fish because they eat mosquito larvae and are fun to watch.

To keep your fish from becoming raccoon dinner, build the pond so that sides drop straight down at least 2½ feet (which rules out the sloping sides that are safer for young children) or place pieces of wide drainpipe on the bottom of the pond so that fish can hide inside.

You may want to think carefully before you add fish, however. They increase the nitrogen load in the water, which can cause algae to flourish. If you just want mosquito control, try letting nature run its course instead of adding fish. Frogs, salamanders, and dragonflies are likely to visit and breed in your pond, and their young also eat mosquito larvae. (Fish will eat all the eggs that the frogs, salamanders, and dragonflies produce.)

If you do get fish, don't overdo it. One or two in a small pond may be plenty. If you want to overwinter fish where winters get very cold, part of the pond should be at least 2 feet deep. Koi need an area that's 3 feet deep. Consider adding a filtering system to prevent an algae problem.

To give your pond a natural look, ring it with stones of different sizes and tuck plants between them. Include plants that will scramble over the stones as well as types that will billow up over them (top). You might want some stones to rise right from the water's edge (left, both views).

DESIGNING A GARDEN POND

To hold water in an artificial garden pond, you can build a concrete shell (expensive and complicated), use a preformed, rigid liner made of fiberglass or polyethylene, or spread out a flexible liner made of a rubber-like material.

Flexible liners are easy to install, and several of the higher-end types carry warranties that last several decades. If cost is the deciding factor, limit your choice to a rigid liner or a less expensive flexible liner, such as one made of PVC (polyvinyl chloride). A rigid liner may be more puncture resistant. But it also may be more difficult to install, especially if it is large.

If you want a naturalistic pond, the borders should curve, perhaps in a kidney shape. Symmetrical or round ponds look formal. If you plan to add rooting types of water plants, include planting shelves—relatively shallow, flat areas—and grow the plants in pots so roots will be just a few inches under the surface.

INSTALLING A RIGID LINER

Placing a rigid liner seems simple enough. But the tricky steps are getting the top rim level and packing fill around the sides so that the liner doesn't buckle as water pushes outward.

1 Clear away sod or weeds from the pond area, as well as the area where you will install stone edging. Set the liner right side up and trace around it into the soil, using a yardstick or a straight stick at a right angle to the ground. Highlight the traced shape with sand or spray paint. Also mark the edges of any planting ledges that are molded into the liner. Set the liner aside.

2 Dig a hole to match the liner's shape, plus about 2 inches in all directions. Remove any stones or sharp roots that poke out. Add about 2 inches of sand to the flat areas of the excavation. Pack the sand and smooth

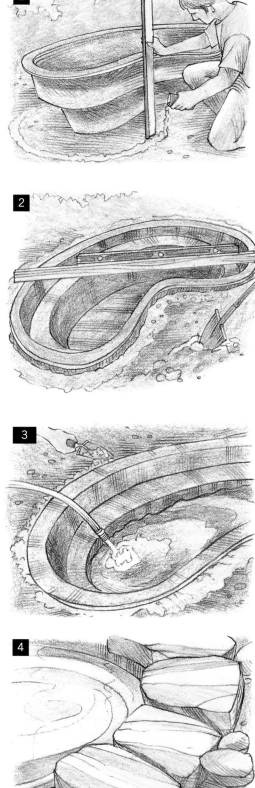

its surface. Set the liner in place. With a carpenter's level, check the top rim in all directions to make sure it doesn't tilt. (If your level won't reach, set a straight 2 by 4 on edge across the liner, and rest the level on that.) If the rim slopes, use some excavated soil to build up the low side.

3 Begin filling the pond with a hose. As it fills, add sand into gaps around the liner. After every 4 inches you add, pack the sand

This newly built small pond is surrounded by plants that will in time grow to partially cover the stone edging.

down with your hands or a stick, but don't push so hard that you lift the liner from the hole. Pace your work so you finish just as the pond becomes full.

4 Shape soil around the pond's edge so that it slopes very gently away from the water. Finish with stone edging (see page 133).

INSTALLING A FLEXIBLE LINER

With a flexible liner, you aren't limited to certain shapes or depths. You can include a gentle slope or build planting shelves at different heights. If you live where raccoons are a problem, you might want to make the shelves wide enough to support big, heavy planters that raccoons can't tip over.

To determine what size liner to buy, decide the maximum depth (usually 2 feet) and double it. Add 2 feet (to allow a 1-foot overlap on edges). Add this total allowance to both the length and the width of your pond. The liner must be at least that big. You might want to order extra to be sure the liner fits.

1 Mark the pond's perimeter with a hose or spray paint and excavate to the depths you want. If you include planting shelves, slope the sides of shelves 1 inch toward the center for every 3 inches they drop. Remove all sharp roots and stones.

Check the rim in all directions by resting a carpenter's level on a 2 by 4. Fill any dips with some of the excavated soil and tamp it down well.

2 Line the hole with liner protection fabric, layers of newspaper, old carpet, or 2 inches of damp sand. With a helper if the pond is large, spread the liner across the hole. (Warming the liner in the sun first makes it more flexible.) Spread the liner so that it has as few creases as possible and rests on the bottom of the hole.

3 Temporarily anchor the edges with heavy stones and begin filling the pond. As the water rises, wade in and continue to adjust folds as the pond fills. Lift the anchor rocks if necessary

to relieve tension on the liner as it settles into place. Allow the pond to settle for a week before you trim the liner and install stone edging. You may also want to water the area with a sprinkler to help compact any soil you loosened and any sand you added around the liner.

ADDING STONE EDGING

The type of edging makes a big difference in a pond's appearance. For a formal look, choose cut stone with uniform joints. For a naturalistic look, use different sizes and shapes. Try to match other stone in your garden, and add plants that cascade over the rocks in some areas so that the rim appears to be only partly ringed by stone.

Stone edging serves two purposes: it gives people a secure place to stand, and it covers edges of the liner. Allow the edging to overlap the water by a couple of inches so that it hides the top

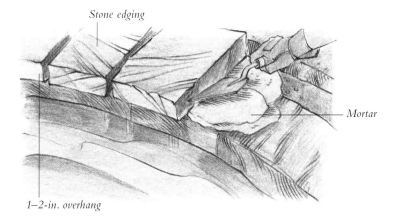

Stone edging

Mortar

1–2-in. overhang

of the liner and shades it from damaging sunshine.

EDGING FOR A FLEXIBLE LINER

Cut excess liner, leaving at least 4 to 5 inches beyond the pond's edge. The simplest method of edging is to just set the stones along the edge of the liner so that they overlap the water by 1 to 2 inches. Seat each one carefully so that it doesn't wobble. Large stones are much more stable than small ones. Where people will stand, try to use extra-large stones, perhaps 3 feet by 3 feet. They distribute weight away from the pond's edge, a fragile spot.

For even greater stability, use mortar to lock the stones in place. (Be careful not to spill mortar in the water or it will become alkaline. That could require you to drain the pond and refill it before you add fish.)

Remove the stones after you have fit them, spread 1 inch of mortar where they were, and set them back into place. Tap them down with a rubber mallet. Using a straight 2 by 4 and a carpenter's level, check that they are even. Allow them to sit undisturbed for 24 hours.

Prepare fresh mortar and fill the joints. When the mortar stiffens, smooth it with a pointed trowel or a brick jointer. Wipe up smears with a damp sponge. Cover the edging with plastic and keep it damp for three days. Stay off it in the meantime.

EDGING FOR A PREFORMED LINER

To avoid buckling the rim of a rigid liner, fortify at least the area where people will stand. Spread a band of mortar on the soil that is slightly higher than the rim, and set the stones on that, as shown below. Continue the mortar back for the entire length of the stones so that it supports them uniformly. Slice off any excess mortar with your trowel within a few hours.

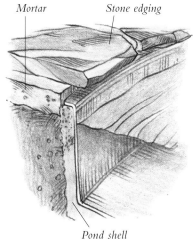

Mortar   Stone edging

Pond shell

LEFT: *If your pond will be viewed from a distance, you can edge it with relatively small stones. Where you expect foot traffic, use larger slabs.*

ADDING STEPPING-STONES

If you plan ahead, you can create a stepping-stone path across your pond. Before you spread the liner, pour a 4-inch-thick concrete footing to support each piece. Then, once the liner is in place, cover each spot with liner protection fabric and set the stepping-stones in place.

If you want to use relatively thin stones in deep water, mortar bricks or blocks to create support posts and place the stones on top. Pavers 1½ to 2 inches thick work well. Mortar increases the alkalinity of water, so if you want to add fish, test the pH level

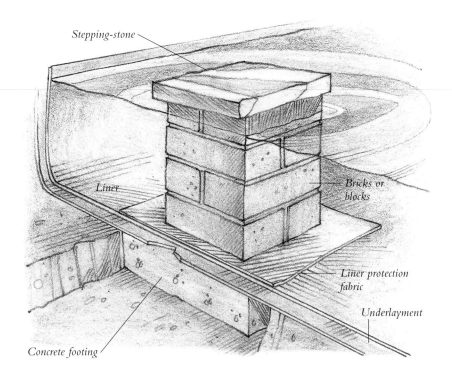

first with litmus paper or a tester kit. For koi, a pH reading of 7.5 is ideal. Companies that sell fish can advise you on how to alter the pH.

PLACING BOULDERS IN A POND

There's something very appealing about having a boulder at the edge of a pond. But most garden ponds don't have edges built to take this weight. You can pour a concrete foundation under the stone, but an even easier solution is to set the boulder either outside the pond or within it. If you put it outside, protect the pond edge from

If you want stone pavers to create a mini bridge across an artificial stream, leave spaces between the foundation blocks so that water can run between them.

The liner must extend all the way underneath boulders that rise directly out of the water. Place liner protection fabric over the liner so it doesn't puncture.

crumbling by disturbing as little of the soil as possible. Choose a low, dome-shaped boulder, if possible, because it will look natural even with its base only a few inches underground.

To add a boulder to the bottom of the pond or to a wide planting shelf, put extra liner protection fabric over the area first. If the boulder has sharp edges, spread round gravel over the protection fabric and put the boulder on top of that. Be very careful not to rip the liner when you position the boulder.

CREATING A BEACH

A beach works best on a pond with a gradually sloping side or a wide, shallow shelf next to an edge. Adding a ridge where the shelf drops into deeper water (see illustration) helps keep the beach material from disappearing into the bottom of the pond. If you want to tuck plants into the beach area, create depressions before you add the liner so that you can add pockets of planting soil on the water side later.

Flexible liner

Planting area in trough on gentle slope

Ridge

Wide shelf

streams

An artificial stream is another great way to incorporate stone into your garden. You have a lot of leeway here: the stream can link to artificial ponds or exist on its own. You can use a pump and hidden water reservoirs to fill it with flowing water, or opt for a dry creek. With or without water, essential features include a meandering route, a mix of gravel sizes, and appropriate streamside plants. A bridge or stepping-stones are optional embellishments.

Building a stream with water is similar to installing a pond with a flexible liner. But instead of one pond, you need two, separated by a liner-lined creek with a very gradual slope, ideally about 1 inch for every 5 to 10 feet. This type of stream is flat enough so that it still holds water when the pump is off, which protects the liner from damage by the sun. If you don't want to see ponds at both ends of the stream, install a covered tank at one or both ends.

Choice and placement of stones determine the overall effect of an artificial stream, whether or not it holds water. Facing page, lush plants soften the look of what started out as a rock-lined channel. At top right, a dry stream features large rocks that jut out into the streambed, just as they often do in rushing streams on mountainsides. Another dry stream (middle right) looks more placid, as if water wore down the stones over time. Below, a rushing stream comes complete with jagged rocks and a few low waterfalls.

waterfalls

With their motion and sound, waterfalls heighten the pleasures of strolling through a garden. A little waterfall produces a soothing sound, while a large one evokes memories of glorious mountain hikes.

You can fine-tune the sound to suit your personal preference. Options include raising or lowering the height of the spillway, turning the pump volume up or down, dividing the flow into two streams by setting a heavy stone on the spillway, or adding stones below the spillway to make a bigger splash at the base of the falls.

Beyond the sensual effects, waterfalls serve several practical purposes. Cascading water picks up oxygen as it mixes with air, which helps make the pond below a healthier place for fish to live. And the motion deters mosquitoes seeking a place to lay eggs.

LEFT: *Although most waterfalls attempt to mimic natural scenes, they don't have to. This waterfall is clearly artificial, yet the grotto-like structure blends in beautifully with a naturalistic pond surrounded by lush growth.*

Naturalistic waterfalls look best when they're built of stone similar to other pieces used around the pond. The spill stone can be a slab like other slabs (top) or a block like other blocks (inset). In multi-stage waterfalls edging can consist of relatively small, jagged stones (far left) or huge, rounded boulders (left) that make the falls seem like the ribbons of water that cascade over cliffs into mountainside meadows.

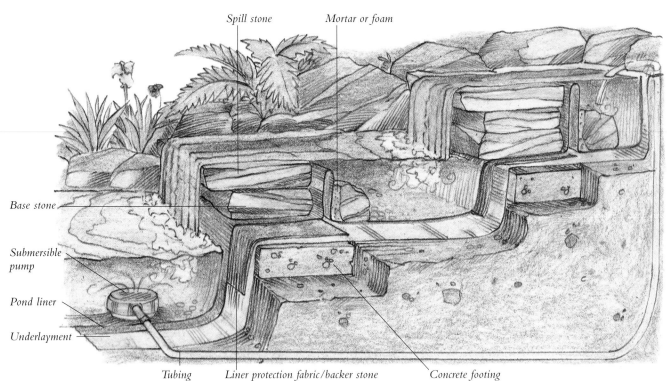

Spill stone   Mortar or foam

Base stone

Submersible pump

Pond liner

Underlayment

Tubing   Liner protection fabric/backer stone   Concrete footing

BUILDING A ONE-STEP WATERFALL

A simple waterfall has a single step, with the water flowing from an upper pond (often hidden) over a spill stone into a lower pond; a pump moves the water through flexible tubing back to the top. This design fits the scale of a small garden much better than a towering waterfall would. And its sound is more relaxing. Because the top reservoir is usually out of view, it's a good place to install a filtering system, if you want to add one to your pond to prevent algae growth.

If you are building a pond and waterfall at the same time, use a single liner, as shown in the illustration above. To add a waterfall to an existing pond, use the following directions:

A one-step waterfall can lead to a pond or an artificial stream.

1 Remove enough water and edging from the pond so that you can pull back the liner where you want the waterfall. If the soil there is soft, reinforce it by pouring a 4-inch concrete foundation that extends slightly above the normal water line of the pond.

2 Without damaging the edge of the pond, create the rough shape for the waterfall area. Depending on your site, you will need to either add or dig out soil. Create a channel wide enough to hold the water-fall stones as well as stones that will line the channel on both

Increasing a waterfall's height increases the sound of the flowing water.

sides. Behind the waterfall, make a depression for the upper reservoir.

3 Smooth the pond liner back into place, over the concrete. Top this with a new liner that's big enough to cover the entire waterfall area, including the channel and the reservoir.

4 Put a piece of liner protection fabric on the liner and set the backing stone in place. Add a spill stone. Ideally, it should have a slight dish shape and a relatively sharp front edge; water flowing over a rounded edge doesn't produce the neat cascade that most people want in a waterfall.

5 Crease the liner behind the waterfall so that the waterproofing extends almost to the top of the spill stone. Use backer stones to anchor the liner so that the crease stays in place. Then spread the liner so that it hugs the ground over the channel and reservoir.

6 Pile up taller rocks on both sides of the backer stones and waterfall to form a channel for the water that looks as if it was naturally scoured. Then set aside the stones, except for those needed to keep the crease in place. Prepare a bagged mortar mix and reinstall the edge stones in a bed of mortar. Also use mortar to plug gaps between stones. Or, instead of mortar, you can use black polyurethane foam designed for use around ponds. (It's similar to the yellow material used to fill gaps in buildings.)

7 Attach flexible plastic tubing to the pump. Put the pump in the lower pond and run tubing to the top pond. Hide the tubing under soil, plants, or stones. Turn on the pump to test the waterfall effect. You may need to tilt the spill stone forward to get the water to run off in a sheet.

8 When you are satisfied with the placement of the stones, run the waterfall for a while to check for leaks. Then shut off the pump. With mortar or foam, permanently set the backer stone and the anchor stones behind the waterfall. Also attach the spill stone to the base stone and fill all gaps.

DESIGNING A MORE COMPLEX WATERFALL

More complex waterfalls are multiples of a simple one, with a series of holding ponds and spillways feeding eventually into a pond where a pump pushes the water uphill so gravity can carry it down again.

The bigger the waterfall, the more it needs really large stones in order to look properly proportioned. Most large waterfalls are constructed with the help of heavy machinery. They also require more piping and a bigger pump.

A Ready-made Waterfall

Instead of piecing together your waterfall with liner and stone, you can buy several types of ready-made waterfalls. Some consist of liners with steps molded in, while others include a holding basin, filtration system, and spillway. These triple-duty products eliminate the need to install a separate reservoir above the waterfall.

141

Credits

(R = Right; L = Left; T = Top; B = Bottom; M = Middle)

DESIGN

Patrick Anderson garden: 85; **Suzanne Arca:** 4, 42T; **Arentz Landscape Architects:** 7T, 81TR, 139TR; **Jeff Bale:** 9BR, 11R, 37, 108TL; **Kirsten Berg:** 39TR; **Elspeth Bobbs:** 123TR; **Jaquie Tomke Bosch:** 43B; **Michael Buccino:** 101TR; **Duncan Callicott:** 115; **Carlotta in Paradise:** 61B; **Chanticleer Garden:** 9TR, 61T, 71L, 101MR; **Bob Clark Design:** 55R; **Clinton & Assoc.:** 76; **Linda Cochran:** 26T; **Conni Cross:** 102B; **Margaret de Hass van Dorsser:** 53TL; **Dickson DeMarche Landscape Architects:** 11L; **Marcia Donahue, sculpture:** 96; **Brad Dunning:** 74BL; **Julian Durrant/Hendrikus Group:** 139TL; **Peter Eastman garden:** 127TL; **Glen Ellison Design:** 49, 59L, 74TR, 94TR, 137B, 139BL, 140; **The Ellsworth garden:** 90T; **Susan Epstein garden:** 141; **Elizabeth Everell Design:** 109T; **Ferguson & Shamamian Architects:** 58; **Feyerabend & Madden Design:** 127TR; **Cevan Forristt:** 99BL; **Ryan Gainey garden:** 128TL; **Antoni Gaudi:** 81MR; **Judith Glover, RHS Chelsea 2003:** 35BR; **Gossler Farm Nursery:** 25TL; **Melanie Green:** 133; **Chris Grey-Wilson:** 24; **Grizzly Landscape Design:** 75B; **Ground Xero Design:** 13BL; **Richard Haag:** 139BR; **Donna Hackman:** 10TL; **Nancy Hammer:** 5B, 6; **Harland Hand:** 104T; **Lucy Hardiman, garden:** 117, 122R; **Bill Harris:** 91TR; **Robert Howard:** 84; **Jane Hudson & Erik de Maeijer, RHS Chelsea 2004:** 34R; **Hyde Hall, Essex:** 23BL; **Virginia Israelit:** 96; **Barbara Jackel Landscape Design:** 129TL; **Chris Jacobson:** 123B; **Johnsen Design & Planning:** 9TL; **Lady Farm, Chelwood, Somerset:** 23TR; **Mia Lehrer + Associates, Landscape architect:** 58; **Little & Lewis, water feature:** 122R; **Mamey Hall, RHS Chelsea 2003:** 136; **Ron Mann Design:** 52L; **Tom Mannion:** 122L; **Ken Mark Landscaping:** 75TR; **Stephen Morrel:** 92; **Martin Moskow:** 128BL; **Jennifer Myers:** 70; **Ernie & Marietta O'Byrne:** 89BL, 125BR; **Oehme, van Sweden & Assoc.:** 135; **Ondra garden:** 71BR; **Ben Page & Assoc.:** 118; **Jack Peterson, masonry:** 117; **David Pfeiffer:** 72L; **Piedmont Designs:** 60; **Tish Rehill & Michael Daugherty garden:** 80; **Cynthia Rice:** 59TR; **Rogers Gardens Colorscape:** 73BR; **Jana Ruzicka, Hortulus:** 98; **Michael Schmidt:** 91MR; **Robert Schultz:** 63T; **Michael S. Smith, Inc., tile:** 58; **Stout garden:** 134; **Peter Strauss:** 25TR; **Freeland & Sabrina Tanner Design:** 90T; **Taormina garden:** 73BR; **Rose Tarlow:** 79; **Philip Thornburg:** 129BR; **Tichenor & Thorp:** 77TL; **Suzanne van Atta:** 89T, 90B, 93B; **Thomas Vetter:** 71TR; **Penny Vogel & Millie Kiggins:** 23L; **Ron Wagner and Nani Waddoups:** 18B, 35TR; **Roger Warner Design:** 137TR; **Phillip Watson:** 10BL; **John Wood, Hampton Court, 2003:** 68L; **Zen Gardens, Yoshihiro Kawasaki:** 106; **Robin Zitter:** 51BR, 56, 128, 144

PHOTOGRAPHY

Warren Agee/Alamy: 104BL; **Brand X Pictures/Alamy:** 30BL; **Marion Brenner:** 21M, 39TR, 52L, 53TR, 55R, 88, 99BL, 101BR, 109T, 127TR, 129TL, 137TR, 137MR, 138L; **Marion Brenner/ PictureArts:** 3, 5T, 40BL, 43T, 53TR, 73L; **Gay Bumgarner/Alamy:** 53BL, 53BR; **Karen Bussolini:** 9TL, 11L, 13BL, 51BR, 56, 59TR, 70, 75TR, 109B, 120, 128, 144; **Rob Cardillo:** 1, 60, 61T, 71BR, 101MR, 134B; **David Cavagnaro:** 31TR; **CuboImages srl/Alamy:** 51MR; **Robin Bachtler Cushman:** 20B; **Arnaud Descat/M.A.P.:** 32; **Andrew Drake:** 8BL, 40TL, 72L, 75MR, 111, 112, 113, 121T, 124T, 139TL; **Miki Duisterhof/PictureArts:** 68R; **Roger Foley:** 7T, 10TL, 63T, 76, 81TR, 91TR, 122L, 135, 139TR; **Garden Picture Library/Alamy:** 34L, 73TR, 105BR; **David Goldberg/Susan Roth & Co.:** 63B; **Steven Gunther:** 98, 101TR; **Neil Hardwick/Alamy:** 51TL; **Pamela Harper:** 97B; **Jerry Harpur:** 10BL, 24, 34R, 35BR, 83; **Marcus Harpur:** 23TR, 23BR, 68L, 136; **Philip Harvey:** 26B; **Saxon Holt:** 4, 9TR, 15T, 21B, 31BR, 42T, 43B, 71L, 89T, 90B, 93B, 104T, 108B, 123B, 125BL, 130, 139BR; **Sandra Ivany/PictureArts:** 11R, 22; **Dency Kane:** 93T, 129BL; **Jacqueline Koch:** 121BL; **Andrew Lawson Photography/Alamy:** 69; **Janet Loughrey:** 23L, 25TL, 26T, 35TR, 41T, 53TL, 71TR, 89BL, 122R, 125BR, 127TL, 129BR; **Allan Mandell:** 5B, 6, 9BR, 18B, 37, 96, 100L, 100R, 106, 107M, 108TL, 117; **Charles Mann:** 13BR, 49, 59L, 61B, 74TR, 75B, 84, 91MR, 92, 94TR, 105TR, 110R, 121BR, 123TR, 128BL, 133, 137B, 139BL, 140; **Steven Nilsson/PictureArts:** 99BM; **Jerry Pavia:** 2, 7BL, 7BR, 12, 16, 18T, 20T, 30TR, 33, 39B, 41B, 44, 50T, 57, 59BR, 65R, 73BR, 80, 81B, 85, 90T, 91B, 107B, 110L, 125TR, 128TL, 141; **Victoria Pearson/PictureArts:** 54, 77TR, 89BR, 108TR; **Norm Plate:** 95BR, 97T, 102T; **Norman A. Plate:** 9BL, 130; **Lisa Romerein/PictureArts:** 94BL; **Susan A. Roth:** 39MR, 81MR, 102BL, 115, 118; **Susan Seubert/PictureArts:** 31ML; **Richard Shiell:** 21T; **Evan Sklar/PictureArts:** 64TR; **Chris Fotoman Smith/Alamy:** 30TL; **Frantisek Staud/Alamy:** 99T; **Neil Sutherland/Alamy:** 99BR; **TH Foto/Alamy:** 50B; **Tim Street-Porter:** 25TR, 38, 58, 74BL, 77TL, 79, 124B; **Tim Street-Porter/ PictureArts:** 31TL; **Jonelle Weaver/PictureArts:** 123TL; **Michele Lee Willson:** 14B, 42B, 62, 116

Index